PETER MACNAB was reared on Mull, as ~~his father, and his~~ grandfather before him. His father retired from colonial service in Hong Kong in 1904 to become Governor of the Mull Combination Poorhouse (Achafraoch House) near Tobermory. Now 94, Peter Macnab, retired from banking since 1963 and still at heart a Mull *teuchter*, has written this fascinating account of Mull during the first quarter of the 20th century against the background of his early years as son of the Governor of the Poorhouse.

Since boyhood he has been an enthusiastic fisherman, and his stories of fishing in lochs and rivers on Mull form an important element of *Tobermory Teuchter*. A keen golfer, once handicap three and past captain of West Kilbride Golf Club, he also makes reference to his very first experiences of the game on the old Tobermory course, where one of the chief hazards was grazing cattle.

Peter Macnab's zest for life and relish for a good story shines through everything he writes. He is a gifted communicator and observer, who loves researching byways of Scottish history. A keen amateur photographer, he was in the right place at the right time when, in 1956 on holiday with his son, he took a now classic picture of the Loch Ness Monster.

Peter Macnab has written, lectured and broadcast about Scotland in general and Mull in particular. Author of a range of books about the island, including the first standard study of Mull and Iona, he is known to lovers of Scottish lore worldwide through his many contributions to the *Scots Magazine*.

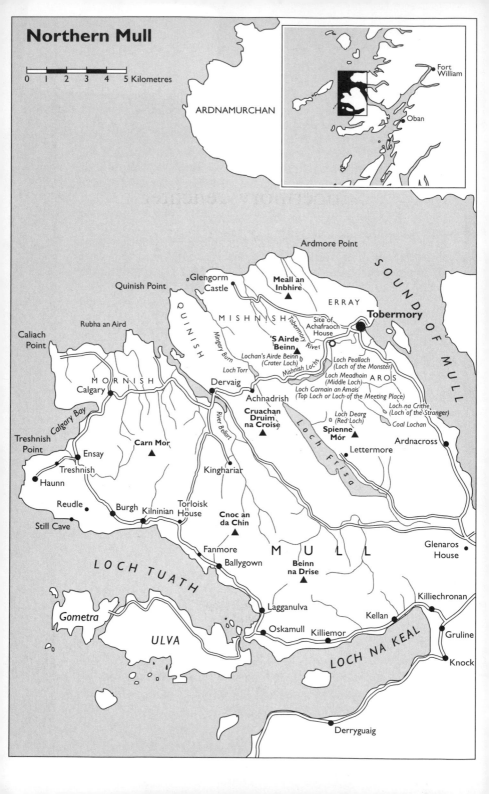

Tobermory Teuchter

A first-hand account of life on the
island of Mull in the early years
of the 20th century

PETER ANGUS MACNAB

Luath Press Limited

EDINBURGH

www.luath.co.uk

First Edition 1998
Reprinted 2003

The paper used in this book is acid-free, neutral-sized and recyclable.
It is made from low chlorine pulps produced in a low energy, low
emission manner from sustainable forests.

Printed and bound by
Bell & Bain Ltd., Glasgow

Typeset in 10.5 point Sabon by
S. Fairgrieve, Edinburgh, 0131 658 1763

Contents

To my family and the memory of happy days;
but especially to granddaughter Louise, who in her love
for Mull is a veritable incarnation of her grandfather!

ACKNOWLEDGEMENTS

With grateful thanks to Luath editor, Catriona Scott, for converting my assorted writings into the impeccably edited book you are about to read, and to my son, Peter, for joining me in my latest 'literary endeavour' by setting the scene in his foreword – given the subject matter of the book, it seems absurd yet perhaps appropriate that the entire text was e-mailed to him on a consultancy assignment somewhere between Aberdeen, Azerbaijan and the Ukraine: the old world meets the new!

Foreword

AS A RECEPTIVE LITTLE BOY I thrived upon father's wondrous tales of a boyhood spent on a remote Hebridean island where lived exciting characters amongst wild mountains and glens full of ghosts. A land full of history of hardship and battle where faraway lochs teemed with fighting brown trout.

By the age of eleven everything fell into place. Staying at Lettermore at the side of Loch Frisa we had a boat to ourselves all day and marvellous bays and islets to explore when the fishing went off. As a strict angling disciplinarian, father ensured that I was brought up in the 'fly only' tradition except where circumstances deemed such a convention impractical. While having to learn the boatman's skills of drifting the boat precisely over a feeding fish I was made to understand that catching trout this way was far easier than casting off the bank. I would not have 'arrived' until I had caught my first trout off the bank, ideally casting into a half gale. And, by golly, I did it that first holiday! A lovely speckled twelve ouncer from a hill loch near Loch Frisa extracted fulsome praise from the master – even although the half gale was absent!

Speaking of half gales I remember we arrived at the Mishnish lochs on the last day of our holiday to find the wind so strong it made fly fishing impossible. Undeterred, father took me to a spot which, he maintained, had never let him down since he was a boy. Putting on some worms, held on with sheep wool, he cast out for us both and laid the rods down side by side. Within 15 minutes he had three beautiful trout of over one pound each on the bank while my rod, a mere foot or two away, remained still. We always remembered that present to him from his favourite loch.

On our many family trips to Mull, often, while my sister, a keen fisher in her own right, and I cast on unproductive waters, father would disappear up the hill to return with a bunch or root of white heather. I have never met anyone else with such a 'feel' for finding white heather in the wildest areas. It's probably a shame that he never had the opportunity to challenge the expertise of the truffle seeking dogs of Italy!

In later years we took the car and camped by our favourite lochs, extra shelter provided by a little ruined roadside crofthouse. Father had enjoyed many a ceilidh there in years gone by and therefore knew the location of the little hidden spring the family had used which provided us with the purest water for our tea!

There was the morning luxury of that first breath of Mull air, heavy, damp after the night's rain and fragrant with bog myrtle and heather. It was then a huge breakfast, sandwiches prepared for lunch and off to the lochs. At the end of the day there was the late evening summer stillness, the western light fading into the summer gloaming and perhaps the far off bleat of a lonely sheep. Then on with the electric light, wired up from the car battery, and twenty minutes bedtime reading, the tent flaps shut and ourselves swathed in silk scarves against the notorious Mull midges.

Having inherited father's craze for fishing I can relate in particular to the chapter on how he learned to fish on his own 'private' river. I am glad to say that Louise, his ten-year-old granddaughter, has also caught the 'bug' and recently caught her first trout! I would add that her mother, Kamala, has proved on occasion a more successful fisher than her father in law!

The description of day-to-day life in the Mull Poorhouse provides a fascinating and unique commentary not only on the inmates but also on the administration and background of how the Poorhouse came into being.

I remember being brought up to stories of the local characters, some of whom I managed to meet when I was a boy, and a number of these and the more printable of the stories feature in the chapter on Local Notables and the MacDougalls of Haunn.

If we were not fishing we were off to explore or to visit father's relations, old friends or new friends who had come to settle from the south. In addition to writing and fishing, father's staggering range of hobbies includes crook-making, golf, photography, horticulture and Mull social history, and he is also a keen amateur geologist. These interests largely dictated our daily schedules as one minute we could be scrambling up a hillside to photograph an elusive view or location of some long ago incident, or be off on a foray to seek an ossified tree or sill of amethysts or perhaps to meet a shepherd to negotiate some ramshorns or scour a hazel wood for sticks to make crooks.

On the other hand, it might be to meet his relations like the Maclean brothers of Dervaig, Betty Maclean's late night suppers alone being worth a trip to Mull, or Maggie MacDougall, or old friends like retired keeper John Macdonald of Tobermory or Donald MacKechnie and Nelly Stewart of Dervaig. They all had the kindness, humour and self-deprecating manner that I have found in my father, although to avoid the prospect of disinheritance I should perhaps glide past his occasional faults which he would anyway attribute to the passing years!

Incidentally, once after ghillieing all day for us on Loch Frisa, that fine Highland gentleman, the afore-mentioned John Macdonald, apologetically asked if we could drop him off in Dervaig where we were staying. The then eighty-year-old did not want to inconvenience us, had thought nothing of walking the ten miles home from Dervaig and was quite embarrassed when we insisted on driving him home!

Father's love of Mull, its people and Tobermory in particular stems from his early days on the island. He has a strong sense of social justice largely resulting from being raised in the Poorhouse as son of the Governor and hearing the harrowing stories of the old people whose families had been left destitute by the Clearances and uncaring Victorian lairds.

As Dux of Tobermory School, he went on to attain six

'Highers' by the age of sixteen at Dunfermline High School. However, having put his elder brother and sister through university, his parents had insufficient resources to enable him to follow his brother's degree in medicine. A life threatening illness thwarted a journalistic career and banking as a less stressful profession was recommended.

Banking never fulfilled his ambitions and he used his natural ability and restless energies to develop the range of social interests and hobbies, many of which he still enjoys, and for which Mull initially proved the ideal medium.

Remembrance through this book for a past way of life and its values is useful when looking at Mull and its relevance today in social and economic terms. The close knit communities and insularity of the earlier part of this century as described by the author have largely gone due to progressive unemployment and improved transport and communications. This in turn has opened up Mull to new generations within the United Kingdom and beyond.

Some of those visitors to Mull have remained to create a new business community to blend with the indigenous local industry. Many of the incomers have successfully met the challenge of earning a living and combating the economic problems of island living, and those who have succeeded have contributed their ideas and talents to supplement those of the indigenous islanders.

However, any remote community requires Government support to remain viable. Nowadays a further complication to living in a harsh and remote environment can be the intrusion of a further layer of governance through the European Community, and argument continues over measurement of the net financial benefit to island communities. Withdrawal or reduction of the agricultural subsidies, for example, would have a devastating effect on the farming community, especially hill farmers. The Government must surely consider some strategic long term plan, in which tourism can play a part, to meet the

EEC shortfall and financial support fluctuations in order to assist those who decide to live and work in remote parts of the country, of which Mull is such a prime example.

This book reminds us that while life on Mull was harsh for many in the old days, the communities, of which the author was a member could still exist. Why should such a land ever become a deserted wilderness for the seasonal pleasures of the few while there are still those who choose to live and work there?

I see the purpose of this book as not merely a snapshot of past times and values but as a reminder and inspiration to build upon these times in order to continue a community life in Mull and the islands for as long as people wish to follow it.

The stresses and problems of modern living together with a new attitude towards the Gaelic culture enhance the attraction of living in the Highlands. By chance, while I was working in Russia last year a colleague proved to be the great-grandson of father's headmaster who threatened to belt any boy caught speaking Gaelic! We remarked upon how these values have changed today for the better.

For many years father has been a passionate salesman for Mull, and Tobermory in particular, in his books, articles, broadcasts and lectures. However, at 94 years old, far from living in the past, he will argue with anyone who will care to listen on why there is an even greater need today to emulate other small countries such as Norway which maintain small communities. He considers the continued viability of Mull and the Highlands and Islands to be a national social responsibility for as long as people wish to live and work there and in so doing maintain something at least of the Gaelic culture which was officially discouraged in his youth and which through his writings he has tried in some way to preserve.

Peter Alexander Macnab
May 1998

Introduction

THE FIRST 25 YEARS of the 20th century in Mull were a period of slow transition from the years of Victorian landlordism towards the age of progress, sophistication and permissiveness. I realise that I am now probably unique, having spent that quarter century in Mull, first as a schoolboy before, during and after World War I, and then as an apprentice banker, learning about and absorbing every facet of society, from the lives of the descendants – or survivors – of the Clearances and the social and financial affairs of the community, to the business of the land-owning gentry. Lacking all the amenities that today are taken for granted, what did we do then and how did we live? We created our own pastimes and interests, and community and domestic life was simple and uncomplicated.

The author with his son, right, and, left, Donald MacKechnie of Dervaig,
an authority on Mull folklore. 1973

In the following pages I shall try to present a picture of Tobermory and the Isle of Mull in peace and war and perhaps draw some comparisons between then and now. Why I refer so much to Tobermory and the north of Mull, rather than the whole island, is because the picture has to be rather local, for in those days, when communications on the island were so difficult, each township tended to be a close-knit community with a high degree of insularity. Why, it was almost as easy to reach Glasgow or Edinburgh by mailboat and train as it was to reach Iona which was 50 miles distant by road at the other end of the island. My father used to say that when returning on home leave from Hong Kong, the worst part of the journey was the bit between Oban and the north of Mull!

The author in the 1950s

My father and his forbears were Mull people. When he retired from the post of Superintendent of the Hong Kong Police Force in 1904, and felt a natural urge to return to the land of his birth, he accepted the vacant post of Governor, with my mother as Matron, of the Mull Combination Poorhouse (known later as Acha-fraoch House) at Tobermory. We moved there in 1906 when I was three years old.

Peter Angus Macnab
May 1998

CHAPTER I

Life at the Mull Combination Poorhouse

THE MULL COMBINATION POORHOUSE, latterly renamed Achafraoch ('Heatherfield') House, was opened in 1862. In the middle of the 19th century the full impact of the Clearances took effect. Local authorities – the Parish Councils – began to realise that the financial support for so many destitute, old and infirm people was placing such an increasing burden on the ratepayers that something had to be done to ease the situation. (I do not think we appreciate the financial acumen of the local treasurers of the 1850s.) Working out the cost per head and equating that to some form of centralised care, they decided that the building of poorhouses was the answer for Poor Relief (the DHSS of yesteryear). Accordingly, poorhouses were built

The Mull Combination Poorhouse – Achafraoch House – in 1920

in areas such as Skye, Oban, Lochgilphead and Tobermory, each financed by a consortium of local Parish Councils whose responsibilities covered some of the worst-hit areas of the west.

The Mull Poorhouse was built at a cost of £20,000 by a consortium of the three Mull parishes, together with Moidart, Morvern, Ardnamurchan, Coll and Tiree, each parish sharing in the subsequent maintenance cost in proportion to the number of inmates accepted from each.

The building was erected on the south side of the river, over a mile from Tobermory, beside the road to Dervaig. A drystone boundary wall enclosed an area of five acres through which flowed the Tobermory River. Such was the greed of the landowner, that the annual feu duty payable to the superior – Aros Estate – was immediately raised to £29 from 12/6 (62¹/₂p), its original grazing value as rough hill land.

The rambling establishment had two storeys, one wing for male inmates, the other for female. It was built with the hard basaltic stone that was quarried from what had been a heathery little mound behind where the house was built. The sandstone window facings were brought in from elsewhere.

Decisions with regard to admission lay in the hands of the Inspector of Poor, Coundullie (or Cowan) Morison – a welfare officer, as we would describe him in modern times – who was also treasurer of the Committee of Management. Ironically, the Committee was composed almost entirely of the lairds, many of whom were the very men whose acts had brought about the need for the provision of such a building – at the public expense.

Some of the poor would have preferred to live in squalor and misery in their own homes in order to remain independent, and regarded the Inspector of Poor with resentment when he ordered their admission to the Poorhouse for their own good; not that they lost their independence, for they could leave at any time if they could look after themselves or be accepted by relatives. This happened on a few occasions, but it was sad to see people re-admitted if they had resorted to their old ways.

The planners of the poorhouses deserve praise for their foresight. It was not a case of dumping the folk inside, feeding and clothing them, to wear out what was left of their lives. On the contrary, everything was done to preserve their will to work on a voluntary basis, encouraging the fit to discharge themselves if an opportunity to work presented itself in the community. The poorhouse was really a combination of two of the type of units we have today, a rehabilitation centre for the able-bodied and a home for the aged.

The author and his family in 1909 in front of Achafraoch House

The Mull Combination Poorhouse was built to accommodate 100 to 130 people, men and women. By the early years of the 20th century the numbers had dropped considerably, and three upper wards in the men's wing were altered and divided to provide excellent living quarters for the governor and his family consisting of a 'parlour', sitting room, four bedrooms, kitchen-livingroom, etc. The outlook was to the east, towards the entrance gates, with a distant view of a small stretch of the Sound of Mull and the hills of Morvern beyond.

The inmates assembled in the large dining hall for meals and for the religious service on Sundays, the men on one side, the women on the other. The Sunday service was usually in the Gaelic, delivered from a pulpit in the dining hall by the Reverend Donald Bell, minister of the Baptist Church in Tobermory, who was appointed to watch over the religious side of the establishment.

There was very little comfort as we would see it today. There were hard benches. Any form of seat or padding was reserved for victims of arthritis, of whom there were many after lives of hardship. The fires in the Victorian iron framed fireplaces were small and often fed with heather and scraps of wood picked up around the place. One must remember that these were people who in their lives had been inured to hardship, and they probably found the conditions luxurious compared with their previous environment. Clean clothes were always available, and comfortable beds. The mattresses were filled with straw: rustling, sometimes lumpy, but very warm, and replacement was easy in the case of ill health or incontinence.

In the early years of my parents' appointment there were about 35 men and women. The number fell sharply after the year 1909, when Lloyd George introduced the Old Age Pension of 5/- per week for the over-70s. This allowed many families to take in and care for elderly relatives because they would no longer be a financial burden. In one of Neil Munro's Para Handy tales he tells of the old woman, a poor widow, on her way to the poorhouse at Lochgilphead. On being told about the new Act and the Old Age Pension, she exclaimed: 'Fife shillings a week! I hope I'll be as weel off

The author's mother and father in 1920

when I get to Heaven!' That gives some idea of the reaction of old people to the windfall. I can't resist following that up with another of Neil Munro's stories, this time about a 'Pensioners' Farm'. 'There was a man who had the idea of collecting a herd of chenuine Macleans from Mull, not one under seventy, and he fed them on the potatoes they grew for him, and oatmeal he bought in bulk, making a nice living for himself off their pensions that he collected. His worry was that they would keep trying to run away on matrimonial adventures!'

The staff in the Poorhouse consisted of a porter-handyman, a cook and two maids, but this was reduced as the years went on and the numbers of inmates decreased, until the place became more of an old folks home. Wages, with all-found, were 10/- (50p) per week for the maids, and slightly more for the cook and porter.

Forming part of the main building was a one-storey extension containing a barn, a woodstore, three north-facing stores
for paraffin, milk and perishables, meat and fish, and a big
kitchen with a huge range that swallowed coal but gave a steady
supply of hot water throughout the house. The cook's room led
off the kitchen. Beyond that lay the big scullery, coalhouse,
laundry and drying room. At the far end was the mortuary, with
its grim, white-washed walls.

There was an enormous mangle in the laundry that had
heavy weights that thumped up and down and required a lot of
energy to turn the handle. There were also several large tubs
that were kept for washing blankets in the summer with the
soft water from the burn. Left temptingly close to the long pool
behind the house, they were irresistible to young boys as a
source of adventure. We launched the tubs and sailed off one
by one on our voyages of discovery, although not without some
trepidation as we pulled ourselves across the water by means of
the old fence stretched across the burn. This was once too tame
for one of our number who expressed his contempt at our
timidity. Pushing off into the deeper reaches of the pool, he
paddled himself along with a piece of plank. Standing up, the
more effectively to increase the pace, he overbalanced, and the
tub up-ended and squirmed like an angry tortoise, then tilted
back again as our bold friend stood up spouting in about three
feet of water. We had to build a big fire with heather stalks in
the quarry to dry some of the burn water out of his clothes.

For domestic purposes we had an excellent supply of
water piped from a spring half a mile distant above the wood
behind the house, cold and refreshing after its long journey
through the boglands. Within the house most of the piping
was of lead, yet we had no cases of deaths or delirium
through lead poisoning!

There was a well-built stable, a byre and a three-pen pig-
gery. Pigs were no longer kept when the reduced numbers of

inmates meant fewer scraps. The other building would have housed a horse and cows in the early days, but when we lived there it served as a henhouse with rows of perches. Nor was this all: there was a separate blacksmith's shop with every conceivable tool for field and smithy. The porter's lodge stood beside the tall, wide, front entrance gate. It was no longer occupied by the porter but used as a store, with a joiner's shop and even a shoemaker's bench. The porter was more comfortably accommodated within the main building.

There were large walled gardens for vegetables and soft fruits and for relaxation areas for inmates. The outer fields, won originally from heather and bog, were now productive, growing potatoes, hay, oats and kail. Surplus crops were sold locally and the money put towards maintenance costs. Able-bodied inmates, under the supervision of the porter, prepared the ground and helped with the harvest, although sometimes

The author's father, mother and sister having a break during hay harvesting in 1918

9

a horse-drawn plough on hire was available. Threshing the oats with the flail was winter work for the porter. The women helped with the washing-up and laundry work. There was never any compulsion, and the folk seemed pleased to have something to do.

Meat, fish and groceries were delivered by Tobermory merchants, and milk came from the nearby farm of Sgiobruadh. Coal was delivered by the ton load and cost 10/- pre-World War 1 – the price escalating with inflation.

In the lavishly equipped dispensary was an array of bottles of all shapes, sizes and colours, containing, according to the names etched on the fronts, enough cyanide and associated poisons to have wiped out the population of Mull. In the early days, of course, doctors had to prepare their prescribed medicines with their own hands. Dr Morison from Tobermory paid a weekly visit of inspection, as it was a statutory duty for the inmates to be visited once a week by a doctor.

A view of Achafraoch House taken from the east showing 'The River'. The Governor's quarters occupy the top flat of the main building. The bell hanging high on the left-hand wall was used to summon the inmates to meals and church service.

If one considers the general housing conditions in 1862 when Achafraoch House was built, the sanitary arrangements in the building were reasonable. Baths were essential, and there were four, one up and one down in each wing of the house, but toilet facilities were somewhat lacking, consisting of one cubicle and wash-hand basin in each of the men's and women's wings. However, there was the old-fashioned dry lavatory provision in the outhouses, with a line of wooden seats for each sex and the appropriate iron containers below. The sewerage system was good, the effluent being carried far into an almost inaccessible bog half a mile distant.

All illumination was by paraffin lamps and candles in a variety of holders. This was one charge my father laid on himself for daily supervision: the correct trimming of wicks, globe cleaning and careful paraffin replenishment.

The grim picture of life in the poorhouse presented by Charles Dickens that exists in people's minds was in no way representative of our establishment. Well sheltered, well cared for, well clothed, with ample and varied food, and health care, the inmates' contentment was obvious, especially when they could be heard joining together in song and exchanging old stories. From our rooms we often heard the faint voices of the men, rising in a Gaelic chorus from their common room down below. One song sung to a Gaelic air was a satire on the Inspector of Poor, reflecting on the personality of Cowan Morison and the fine Tam o' Shanter he wore:

With a rumbling, tumbling, hey bonny lass;
With a rumbling, tumbling, m'ceannsach;
With a rumbling, tumbling, hey bonny lass,
Tammy shanter aline m'ceannsach.

The diet was plain, but ample and varied, eaten off ringing and easily washed tin and enamelled tableware. There were

GROUND PLAN

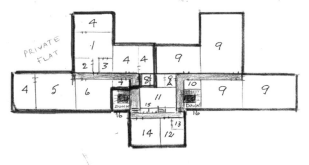

FIRST FLOOR

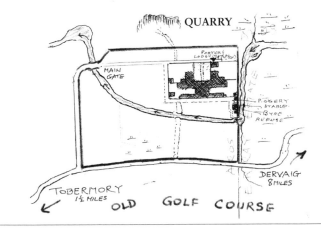

Ground Floor Plan

1	Main Entrance
2	Office
3	Spare Room
4	Linen, Clothing
5	Bathrooms
6	Men's/Women's Day Rooms
7	Side Wards
8	Toilets
9	Main Wards
9A	Porter's Room
10	Spare Side/Bedroom
11	Stairs
12	Mens' and Womens' Outside 'Dry Closets'
13	Dining Room
14	Main Kitchen
15	Meal etc Store
16	Scullery/Wash-up
17	Cook's Room
18	Milk Store
19	Meat/Fish
20	Paraffin (Lighting)
21	Barn (Oats storage)
22	Store
23	Wood Store
24	Blacksmith
25	Coal Store
26	Laundry
27	Drying
28	Ironing
29	Mortuary

Private Flat

1	Kitchen
2	Larder
3	Coal, etc
4	Bedrooms
5	Parlour
6	Sitting Room
7	Pantry/Dishwash
8	Bathroom/Toilet

Empty Wards, etc

8A	Unused Bathroom/Toilet
9	Empty Wards
10	Disused Pantry
11	Dispensary (Medical)
12	Fever Ward
13	Do. Wash Basins etc.
14	Maids' Room
15	Maids' Toilets
16	Stairs

NOTE:- The whole building was divided along the centre from the main entrance to dining room: men – left side (North); women – right side (South). Inmates met only at meal times on opposite sides of the dining room. There was no provision for married quarters; the occasion never arose to my knowledge. The normal staff complement was: two maids; one cook; one porter/handyman.

Fit inmates worked – the men in the fields and gardens, the women in the laundry.

great mugs of tea, slabs of thick bread and cheese, porridge, soups, boiling beef varied by helpings of salt cod or herring, steeped overnight to avoid too salty a taste. Home grown vegetables were abundant. There was even a weekly supply of tobacco for the smokers, including a few of the women who also enjoyed a puff. I used to watch my father chopping off each ration from a big roll of Bogey Roll tobacco which looked like a coiled snake. There were clay pipes available (these were still in general use in the early days of the century). The men often eked out their ration by the addition of some dried roots and plants. My father sometimes lit his pipe with Fusee matches, something of a luxury; these had a long-lasting spluttering head, designed to light the pipe under windy conditions. There was always a risk if the smoker had luxuriant whiskers.

The big day of the year was Christmas. The suppliers in Tobermory would subscribe to provide a really impressive dinner, perhaps the only occasion on which the men and women were allowed to meet and fraternise. Some of the lairds on the Committee would call at the house, and give a small present and a glass of *uisge beatha* to the old folk which brought a Gaelic blessing from them and a sparkle to their eyes.

With regard to the high incidence of arthritis, some of the men used to go over to the bogs and collect the leaves of the bog bean which grew on the pools. From these they infused a brew said to be very helpful for the sufferers. In the days of the kelp industry, when the coastal dwellers collected vast heaps of seaweed, to be dried and burned for the production of the kelp ash, it is recorded that never before or since was the incidence of rheumatic disorders so rampant. Wading in the sea in all conditions, the clothing of those people was seldom dry.

There was a grisly tale of one old man who had died so crippled and deformed with arthritis that in the mortuary his body had to be securely kept horizontal by the addition of heavy weights The Tobermory joiner sent his new apprentice to take the necessary measurements. It was a very windy day, and on entering the white-walled little room with its sheeted occupant, the boy left the door open. As he was about to carry out his duties with the footrule there came a great gust of wind ... the door slammed shut, and the vibration dislodged the weights. The corpse jerked up and the sheet slipped partially off. Fortunately for the youth the handle of the door did not come off in his frenzied clutch, and he beat all Olympic records back to the joiner's shop where he finished up cowering under the bench. I was told this story many years later, thank goodness, otherwise my youthful imagination might have been disturbed, to say the least!

A person's end was mostly quiet and reverent, with the

The very last inmates of Achafraoch House. They were transferred to Oban on the closure of the Poor House in 1923.

The ruins of Achafraoch House in 1960 before its demolition

doctor and minister in attendance if possible. Interment took place seven miles over the hill at Kilmore Cemetery, Dervaig, where a plot was set aside for the inmates. The conveyance was a cart, attended by the porter, the minister, my father, and any relative who wished to attend. The lives of these poor folk might have been harsh, but their end was peaceful enough.

As time went on, the poorhouses became an increasingly unjustifiable burden on the rates, for with the steadily decreasing number of inmates, the cost per capita of keeping them going was too high. In fact, Parish Councils realised it would have been better to have provided some less elaborate type of housing and care for the destitute in their own district and in their familiar surroundings. But at the time the poorhouses were built, of course, the problem was so desperate that something had to be done, and what was done served the purpose well.

In 1923, with only four geriatric cases – all men – remaining, Achafraoch House was closed down and the men moved to Oban. The whole unit was sold for £400, and the building, stripped of all its non-ferrous metals, rapidly became a ruin. It was razed to the ground in the 1960s and its stonework conveyed to Tobermory, where it was used to extend a rough jetty out to sea by the Distillery.

The porter's lodge was retained and subsequently modernised, and it has served well as a private dwelling house. Within the original boundary walls the fields still provide good grazing; but the fine agricultural land we knew and cultivated is no more.

CHAPTER 2

Life in Tobermory

ALTHOUGH THE LAST of the Clearances had taken place in Mull in the early 1880s, their effects still lingered in early 20th century Tobermory. There was a lot of hardship, and there were none of today's so-called essential services. In 1920 there were still about half a dozen thatched houses above the school at Glac-na-Ceardach.

Before 1920 there were few motor cars. Until the late '20s there was no electricity. We had the telegraph but no telephone until 1930. There was no television, of course, and radio only came with the introduction of the 'Cat's Whisker' in the late '20s. There were no organised communications within the island. Mail and papers were delivered in the evening.

The last thatched cottages in Tobermory, above the school at Glac-na-Ceardach, 1926

Illumination, including street lighting, was by paraffin, with candles around the house, and latterly the more effective Tilley pressure lamps. A few of the larger houses were lit by acetylene gas, generated by adding water to calcium carbide. In the late 1920s a local electricity supply was provided by harnessing the water of the Tobermory River at the Eas Brae to run a generator in the small building that still stands there.

Tobermory Bay from the Lighthouse path

Although Tobermory had a good supply of water laid on from the reservoir two miles up the Dervaig road (water is drawn today under modern conditions from the Mishnish Lochs), some of the older properties were slow to take advantage of this and water had to be fetched from pumps set up in the town. There were also quite a few 'dry' closets with all their inconvenience.

Domestic duties were fairly onerous, especially with

dependence on fires. Coals and kindling had to be carried and logs chopped, and in some localities there was the heavy job of cutting and preparing peat for fuel.

Family life and existence on the islands depended on sheer hard work. Crofting was an exacting life. The Hebridean islander has an undeserved reputation for some characteristics, one of which is laziness.

> Would that the peats would cut themselves,
> The fish jump on the shore,
> That I upon my bed might lie
> Henceforth for evermore!

But could one blame the people for wanting to rest a bit in the very short periods between seasonal pressures? The fishermen were no better off except that their 'relaxation' was enforced in bad weather. The indigenous island folk were suspicious of change, content to live the old ways in such security as their forefathers had achieved, despite the bitter memories of the Clearances.

These were the days when one still had the instinct to touch the forelock when the 'gentry' went by – they formed an enclave remote from the *hoi polloi*. One of the greatest changes the intervening years have seen is the transformation of most of the old lairds into today's more approachable characters, who involve themselves in local affairs, often under pressure to run their heavily taxed estates as profitable farming units.

Local Entertainment

There was a great deal of 'getting together'. At afternoon tea parties ladies met and exchanged polite gossip over the best china tea service and dainty cakes. There were less formal gatherings in the evenings, when people dropped in for a chat and the news. There were also mini-ceilidhs, with songs and piano accompaniment, when friends were invited. My sister, nine years older than I, was in much demand for her piano renderings of Highland music, when the furniture would be pushed back to make room for dances like *Strip the Willow* or *Petronella*. We played old, now-forgotten games like Catch-the-Ten – the equivalent of bridge.

Magic lantern shows were operated by the distillery manager, Robert Simpson. No matter how often he repeated the slideshow, it never lost its popularity.

I particularly remember how much everyone enjoyed the ceilidhs in the Aros Hall, and the Band of Hope concerts where there would rarely be an empty seat. Songs, piano, fiddle, bagpipes: that was the musical programme, with a few pawky stories related in the Gaelic by some raconteur which rocked most of the audience who understood what he was saying. How I love those simple songs with the rhythm of the swinging oars, the waulking songs with the click of the weaver's shuttle, and not forgetting the haunting love songs. The ceilidhs and concerts were almost always followed by a dance, with lots of lively numbers involving enthusiasm, a lot of perspiration, and recognised steps and formations now partly forgotten. So energetic were they that some characters made this a legitimate excuse to slip out of the hall for a sip at the flat bottle discreetly hidden in their coat pocket. Modern dancing was late to reach the island communities.

During those gatherings, how we youngsters wriggled with delight when the lads of the village came crowding in from the bar next door, redolent with spirits both high and alcoholic, sitting themselves down noisily in the back seats and interrupting the proceedings. Their enthusiasm reached concert pitch if a singer began a popular song such as *Fear a' Bhata* (*The Boatman*). The lads would join lustily in the cho-

rus with such a variety of keys and tempos and the thunder
of heavy working boots (Para Handy once remarked that he
'hadn't his singing boots on'), that they quite drowned out
the singer and the piano, bringing the rendering to an embarrassing halt. The chairman would bellow for order, threatening the over-enthusiasts with expulsion from the hall, if necessary by the strong-armed policeman who always stood
strategically at the entrance door. Amid *sotto voce* remarks in
the Gaelic on the paternity of both the chairman and the constable, the boisterous interlude would end and the concert
resume.

View of Tobermory

While today the ceilidh-concert still attracts big audi-
ences, its character has changed, particularly the music, both
on stage and for accompanying the dance. The old piano-fid-

dle combination has been replaced by the guitar and the drums with a touch of blaring brass. Singing has mostly lost its traditional, often unaccompanied sound, particularly since the advent of microphones.

The Band of Hope recitals were highly popular with us school children, even if we had to recite in unison and in public a rehearsed chorus about the evils of strong drink. We were encouraged to do so by the fact that we each received an apple and an orange for our efforts.

Excellent impromptu concerts were given by the crews of the naval vessels that used to pay Tobermory a courtesy visit every summer, the units ranging from the old *HMS Colossus* to cruisers and destroyers. In return for the friendly hospitality extended to them by the local people, the crew would give a real lower deck variety concert. There were many talented performers, and such a concert could be the event of the year!

The Church

At the turn of the century there were four churches in Tobermory: the Church of Scotland or the 'High' Church up the brae, the Baptist Church on the waterfront near the Distillery (now a museum), the United Free Church, and the Free Church with its impressive spire and rose window. Closed now are the Baptist Church and the Free Church. The United Free Church is a meeting place for the Tobermory Evangelistical Fellowship, and there is a small United Free congregation. The Church of Scotland remains active, and its minister travels around, conducting services in outlying districts where congregations have been combined into more compact units.

This is a far cry from pre-Reformation days when there were at least fourteen chapels on Mull radiating the influence of St Columba and Iona, and from a century ago when every parish had one or more churches and ministers. The people were very religious and also, paradoxically enough, highly superstitious and great believers in the supernatural until education became firmly established.

Distance in those days was no deterrent to going to church. In Wester Ross on the mainland, for example, the people used to walk from Poolewe over the hill road to the church at Gairloch, a distance of five miles, the women in their bare feet until they reached Clach na Brogan ('Stone of the Shoes') above Gairloch. There they donned their footwear out of respect for church and minister.

The Health of the People

At the beginning of the 20th century there were few doctors on Mull. We had only one in Tobermory. There was Dr Reginald MacDonald, who was succeeded by Dr Morison, both of them caring and capable and of the old school.

Doctors at that time were entirely dependent on their own skills and had to be prepared for all emergencies. There was no telephone, and the nearest centre where more medical attention could be found was Oban, but for the patients this would have meant an exhausting journey by the daily mail-boat, or by small ferry boat from Grass Point in the east of the island across the exposed Firth of Lorne. Nowadays, for emergency cases, an ambulance comes by the car ferry from Oban to Craignure to take the patients to Oban Hospital; and for really urgent cases, a helicopter is on call to transfer patients to Oban or Glasgow.

Epidemics of measles, scarlet fever and the more deadly diphtheria occurred regularly, and usually arose from contact with people from outwith the island who were resistant 'carriers' of the diseases to the isolated and susceptible island communities.

The last recorded case of smallpox in Mull occurred in 1891. Smallpox was a dreaded disease, regarded with almost superstitious horror. People would not go near the victims, but would leave food and necessities where they could reach them. The dead were handled in the fumes of burning tar, and would be rolled in a tarpaulin heavily coated with tar as this was the only known safe method of escaping infection.

Health problems were not surprising, particularly among the poorer classes whose houses were damp, sub-standard and crowded, with primitive sanitation; hygiene was difficult to maintain. Under-nourishment was a contributory factor to ill health, and infection spread easily. Consumption, or tuberculosis, was a disease to be dreaded. There was a permanent fear that a neglected cold could end in tuberculosis. Milk was generally of excellent quality, but sometimes its handling was open to suspicion, and the risk of bovine tuberculosis was little understood or heeded.

Most workmen smoked Thick Black or Bogey Roll, strong tobacco that had to be sliced up and ground down between the palms; chewing a plug was not uncommon. However, there was not the wave of death through lung cancer that we experience today with the much lighter and finer tobacco. Certainly, pipe smokers did not inhale the strong smoke. Pipes were usually short-stemmed and foul. A bunch of seagulls' feathers for use as pipe-cleaners was a familiar sight hanging up at the fireside. My father smoked four ounces of strong tobacco a week and we were reconciled to the thick atmosphere created in the living room. I remember my mother placing pot plants infested with greenfly on the shelf beside his chair. It was the pests that died! Smoking was not the cause of my father's death.

Distilling

When I was a boy in Mull there were a few steady jobs. These were mainly in whisky distilling, shop service, sporting estates and domestic service. There was also inshore fishing for lobsters and salmon, and there were important granite quarries in Fionnphort and a marble quarry in Iona. School leaving age was fourteen and unemployment was as much of a problem then as it is now.

Mull's only distillery was at Ledaig, Tobermory, at the foot of the Tobermory Burn whose peaty waters were eminently suitable for the purpose. It was owned then by John Hopkins & Co Ltd of Glasgow who produced the famous Old Mull blend. The distillery gave steady employment to maltsters and others, including peat cutters, for the place was entirely independent. The peats used to be cut at the Mishnish Lochs, whose level was raised by a small dam to ensure a steady flow of water to the distillery under dry conditions.

The distillery bonded store was an impressive building. I remember as a boy seeing bees flying in and out at the upper west corner. When the attic was checked many years later, a huge quantity of old and new honeycombs was found, since generations of bees had taken up residence.

The distillery manager was a family friend, and he told us about a 'secret' operation carried out by some of the workers in the bonded store. When the attention of the excise officer was distracted, they would insert a gimlet into the underside of a stacked whisky cask, bore a tiny hole and catch the trickle of spirits in a tin; then they would tap in a spike of wood, cut it off level with the surface and disguise it with a rub of dust. Sometimes when an old cask was broken up the lower staves would be found to have half a dozen such spikes sticking up through them.

The distillery eventually closed down through crippling

Crakaig, the ruined hamlet in a hollow on the clifftop at Treshnish above the cave
which is the site of an illicit still

taxation, over-production and heavy transport costs. However, in the 1970s it re-opened under new ownership and was completely modernised, but now imports the malt it requires as a more convenient and economic practice. The bonded store has been converted to domestic flats.

Distilling was not confined to authorised premises. Well into the 19th century in many isolated corners of Mull illicit stills were being operated. I have closely examined the remains of what was almost a miniature distillery at the mouth of a convenient dry cave on the shore under the wild cliffs of Treshnish below the deserted township of Crakaig. The operators were skilled (or should it be cunning?) planners. Just inside the entrance to the cave was a semi-spherical 7ft hollow in the centre of a 16ft platform, with a flue built underneath to control the fire below the 'black pot' on which the mixture was heated. The pipe carrying the distillate steam was led under a tiny trickle of water diverted from above, and the resultant spirits caught in a vessel outside. The whole operation was hidden from the sea by a high turf dyke and the smoke was dissipated against the dark cliff. I was told the quality of the product was high, and that the operators even sailed and rowed their way over to Ireland with it where it competed successfully with the local poteen! Some of my forebears were involved in the operation.

The Peats

When I was young peats formed a useful fuel, even with coal costing about 10/- (50p) a ton. One ton of coal has the heat value of 20 tons of peats. In Tobermory one would see stacks of peats at the back doors of some of the houses. Peats are still cut today, but more for the sentimental fragrance than of necessity, for the extraction of peat is labour-intensive, time-consuming and dependent on drying winds.

First the roots of bog myrtle, heather and coarse grasses have to be skinned off to expose the dark peat below, and the darker and usually deeper it is, the better, with centuries of deposits and pressure. The type of spade for extracting the peat varies from area to area. In Mull it has a blade about as long and wide as a block of peat, with a right-angled projecting, cutting edge, with which the peat is cut at an angle, the block then lifted and laid on the surface. When hard enough to be handled (peat contains 90% water), the blocks are set up in little cromlechs or 'tents' through which the drying winds can blow. When thoroughly dry, they are barrowed or carried in creels to the nearest point where a vehicle (horse-drawn in the past, motorised now) can be driven and are taken home to be built into an artistic stack which is then covered with a piece of tarpaulin. A house dependent on peats for fuel would have required a stock of 17,000-20,000 blocks a year, representing at least twenty days of hard work at the midge-infested peat banks.

All hands to the harvest. Haymaking in the early 20s

Mull was once heavily wooded, as far back as the mid-Tertiary Age 40 to 60 million years ago, for the evidence has been found within the rocks, and in the bleached roots of pine trees exposed in the peat. Clearances for early agriculture, climate changes, and wholesale cutting down of woodlands – such as on Torosay estate 200 years ago to produce charcoal for the preparation of explosives for the growing industries of the south – eliminated trees, except within the policies of the mansion houses on large estates, which were the only areas of woodland remaining until after World War 1. Forestry plantings started in 1924 on the Aros Estate and duly expanded elsewhere.

The steady employment of between 70 and 90 men in the forestry industry was welcomed in Mull, especially as it created some casual jobs for crofters and others. Roads had to be improved to carry the heavy loads of timber. The fencing and extending of plantations restricted the freedom of deer to wander and they eventually concentrated in the central and southeast of the island on the stalking estates. The trees planted are usually Sitka spruce and Japanese larch, although as time goes on species of deciduous trees have been introduced.

Farming

During my schooldays more than a dozen crofts were still being worked in and around Tobermory. The crofter could maintain his household and livestock on the produce of his few acres, with the outrun grazings on the hill. Oats were grown, and many houses kept a barrel of local fish, salted or sometimes crudely dried, to supplement the diet. Living conditions were at least adequate.

Every morning and evening on my way to and from school I used to meet the cows going to or returning from the common grazings, chewing their leisurely way along the grassy verges of the roads, often with a collie dog escort which had happily set off on its own to collect them if given the order 'Away and fetch the cows'. The milk cart made its jingling round every morning, and we lingered to gossip with the milkman as he filled our jugs and tins.

The quality of cattle owned by crofters was often rather poor, partly through an adherence to old husbandry methods. According to Frank Fraser Darling, however, Mull with its rich volcanic soil is 'cattle country without equal', but the well subsidised and more convenient sheep have now taken over.

Just after the end of World War i, Sgriobruadh Farm, which had been neglected, was bought by a progressive man, Archie Campbell, who had lost an arm fighting beside the Canadians. He could do as much with his one arm as others could do with two, from ploughing to hair-cutting. In no time

The author's father scything

he had established the best milking herd of cattle in the district. He asked the local crofters why their cows were always picking up and chewing white objects like bones, even pebbles. In reply they simply said that the cattle had always been doing this. As an experiment he set up blocks of salt licks at the stalls in the byre, which the cattle enjoyed. In fact, the best milkers were the best lickers – it was simply a case of a salt deficiency.

Early in the century there were only horse-drawn mechanical aids for farming. The days of the tractor were still to come. Agriculture was labour-intensive. Seaweed which was used for fertilising the ground was brought from the shore either in hand-carried baskets or by horse and cart. Potatoes were lifted by the broad-tined graip. To a great extent grain crops were cut by scythe, a semi-skilled job, although the novice soon acquired the rhythm and the art of sharpening the blade. How often in later years I recalled these lines from *The Scholar Gipsy*, 'With distant cries of reapers in the corn, all the live murmur of a summer's day', as I remembered the sweet scent of new-mown hay, the excitement of the poor rabbit in the final cut, the stooking of sheaves, and then the carrying and storing of them in the barn.

Sometimes we hired a grain separator, but the indoor job in the winter was the threshing of the oat sheaves. This was done with a flail which consisted of two straight lengths of hardwood, such as beech, tied loosely together with a leather thong at one end. The execution was achieved rather like a golf swing, timing the descending swing to strike first on the heads of the sheaves, beating out the ears of grain which filtered through loose boards below. The mixed grain was then winnowed in a strong wind which blew away the light chaff and left the oats to pile up.

CHAPTER 3

Local Notables

TOBERMORY IN THE EARLY YEARS of this century had its fair
share of 'characters', much more so than today's sophisticated and busy inhabitants. What a host of notables I can con-
jure up, from loafers to lairds.

Nicknames are not necessarily cruel or a symbol of pecu-
liarity; they often indicate popularity or identification. In
bank records I have seen a nickname following the correct
designation on an important document as a way of avoiding
confusion. For example, in some small villages, there might

Collecting seaweed from the shore

be a number of 'John Mairs', all customers of the bank. On taking deposits, a nickname could be added to each so that the official title, 'John Mair (Leckie)', or John Mair (Jimsie)', would be unmistakable and accepted by the depositor.

But we schoolboys were a cruel lot and many a nickname, not often complimentary, would emerge from our fertile imaginations. It is interesting how some names arose. In one of our classrooms there were three Donald Macleans from three different families who were referred to as Donald A, Donald B and Donald C. Donald C became contracted to Do'l C which naturally ended up as 'Dossy'. Another youth was known as 'Sleepy' ever after he misquoted the line from the poem of Robert Burns *To a mouse*. In his solo recitation he misquoted the line 'To thole the winter's sleety drizzle', substituting 'sleepy' for 'sleety'.

But what was the explanation for Pluggy, Blochan, Trolly-bags, or Uiseag (the skylark)? Our austere headmaster was called John Levack, so our Gaelic speakers promptly expressed that, in private, as Leabag – the flounder. Cookstie was the name of the school 'whipper-in' or janitor, one of whose duties was to visit the homes of absentees to make sure that their reason for not being at school was valid.

Among the Tobermory characters was Dondon who would give me a lift to school when returning from the dump with the empty rubbish cart, if our times coincided.

But Ned! Now, there was a notable. Having served on a minesweeper with an English crew during the First World War, he returned home with a most refined English accent; but alas, when in his cups, it degenerated into the broadest local Gaelic. On an unforgettable occasion he walked out of a bar on the waterfront 'with his cap on two hairs', as Para Handy would have said. Instead of turning right along the pavement, he crossed the road in a more or less straight line, and continued to step out into space over the edge of the then

The imperishable Ned, Tobermory 1927

unprotected breast wall. Fortunately the tide was in, and tied up just below him was a rowing boat. He fell into it, more or less uninjured. The mixture of invectives rising from the boat caused windows to fly up and an appreciative crowd to gather.

Neil MacDonald who owned the MacDonald Arms Hotel preferred Gaelic to English and some of his descriptions were rather bizarre. For instance, he referred to a high tide as 'the tide's ashore', and a nice fish he brought home would be a 'trout in full plumage'. He was one of the early motorists, owning a robust Model T Ford which he drove slowly and with such fixed concentration that if he was distracted by a question from a passenger, he would keep driving in a fixed line while he thought about an answer. Many a dislodged signpost and damaged drystone wall were attributed to his over-concentration. The car seemed quite used to his ways and always emerged none the worse.

Stout, genial Senior Baillie Fletcher used to stand outside his emporium next door to what was then the Clydesdale Bank. His favourite expression was 'You see for youseff'. On the high frontage of the emporium were the words in tall letters 'Italian Warehouse'. This was a source of conjecture to us, for we could see nothing Italian about the owner or his merchandise.

A group of local Tobermory worthies, the author third from the left. Taken in 1925.

Further along the street you might see the well-loved figure of Robert J Brown, owner of that long-established business Archd. Brown & Son which is still in family hands. He was always accompanied by his dear wee cairn terrier. That dog so loved the Reverend Donald Bell, the minister of the Baptist Church, that whenever they met, partly to stake his claim and partly to show his respect, he always raised his leg against the ankle of the Reverend, unless the latter moved quickly out of range.

Perhaps the most colourful character of all (although the adjective is somewhat misplaced) was Dunkie Dubh, or Black Duncan, so-called due to his duties as Burgh Lamplighter: his skin was permanently ingrained with soot and paraffin oil. Street lighting was provided by a few paraffin lanterns set up on posts at some of the street intersections. Dunkie was a familiar figure at lighting-up and extinguishing times with his sack of cleaning rags, a can of paraffin and a short ladder on his shoulder.

Dunkie was one of the most quick-witted in the town. To avoid cleaning and polishing a badly-sooted glass lamp funnel, he might 'accidentally' let it drop and replace it with a new one from his sack. Called before the Burgh treasurer to account for his increased demands for replacements, his explanation, which was accepted with some reluctance, was: 'It's the glass of these new ones we are getting. They're no' strong enough.'

His classic retort came one day when he was standing at the edge of the pier looking down at MacBrayne's Staffa and Iona cruise ship, the *PS Grenadier*. On board was a group of young men. One of them looked up and, pointing to the disreputable Dunkie Dubh, remarked to his friends, 'See that idiot standing up there? Watch me take a rise out of him.' At that time there was a Marconi station on Argyll Terrace in the upper village with an unusually high wireless pole ('The Big Pole', we called it). Pointing up to it and addressing the lamplighter, the young man enquired, 'I say, my man, can you tell me what fruit grows on that tree?' Without hesitation, and respectfully touching his hat, Dunkie Dubh replied, 'Yess inteet sir; electric currents!'

There was also a gentleman known as 'The Duke', on account of his sartorial elegance on occasions, for instance, when he boarded the mailboat heading for Oban on days of market livestock sales. Newly shaved, wearing his fine blue suit and even a collar and tie, and shod in a pair of brown boots a size too small, he carried a raincoat slung over his shoulder on a length of stackrope. But oh, the sad spectacle he made on his return home next day after enjoying the fleshpots of Oban!

There was a man in our congregation in Tobermory who, although a regular church-goer, was very much addicted to alcohol. However, he salved his conscience when he acquired from somewhere a special pocket flask shaped to resemble a bible. During the sermon, when he thought nobody was looking, he would bend down and have a good mouthful, while apparently studying the scriptures.

Dr Morison was known disrespectfully by us schoolboys as 'Bowels', for his questions always concerned themselves with that part of the anatomy. His brother was Coundullie Rankin Morison (always known as Cowan Morison), the Inspector of Poor, and he was a really kenspeckle figure, for he always wore the kilt and a balmoral bonnet at just the correct angle.

One of Tobermory's most famous sons was Bobby Macleod, highly regarded nationwide as an outstanding player of the piano-accordion, especially for his true rendering of Gaelic airs inspired by his father, himself a fine performer on the bagpipes which he used to play for the enjoyment of his clients in the Mishnish Hotel. It is said that all did not go well when Bobby first acquired a piano-accordian and announced to his father his intention of taking up the instrument. This made his father very angry. He tore the instrument out of Bobby's hands, crossed the street roaring 'You're no' going to play that thing in this house', and tossed it into the sea. But Bobby acquired another box and practised in secret, and in the long run ended up his father's pride.

Eight miles over the hill in Dervaig was the MacDonald family who between them ran a grocers shop, the Post Office, the deliveries and the hotel. They were known as the Dallies – perhaps there had been a rumour at some time of a vague connection with the prestigious Daly's shop in Sauchiehall Street, Glasgow. Dervaig owed much to the services they provided. I remember Allan in particular. He used to drive a delivery van round the countryside to visit isolated farms and households far from the shops. We boys were always enticed by his iced Austrian biscuits, but when war broke out, the name suddenly disappeared. I think they are called Empire biscuits today.

Alister Simpson, the only son of a highly respectable friend of ours, was a Jekyll and Hyde character. Unable to hold down

Alister Simpson and his mother in 1928. Alister was a golfer, a deadly shot and a successful angler (in the absence of the keeper).

a job in the South, he returned home to Tobermory to live with his parents, keeping a few dozen hens and doing odd jobs. He used to confide in me as perhaps his only close friend. He was a crack shot and a single-barrelled 16-bore gun was hidden in a stinking sack below the hens' perches. With his keen eyesight and local knowledge, he knew every movement of the two gamekeepers, bewhiskered Fraser of Aros Estate and Jimmy Black, the weather-beaten custodian of Erray. Many a rabbit, hare and game bird fell into his bag and was slipped through the back door of the butchers. I joined him readily in casting a fly on forbidden lochs, secure in the knowledge that he could identify distant unwelcome figures on the skyline in ample time to let us pack up and pedal home on our bicycles.

A legitimate involvement with him was on the golf course, where he was a fair performer. A disastrous heather fire started from the golf course one day and burned for a day and night, devastating a square mile of moorland. My friend told me later how the fire had started. As there was nobody playing on the course at the time and in an honest effort to do some good, he set fire to an unfair hazard of heather intruding on the 5th fairway near the boundary. Unfortunately he misjudged the strength and direction of the wind and the fact that the heath was tinder-dry after weeks of dry weather, and the blaze took off beyond control. Unobserved, he took off as well. However, he joined the team of firefighters who had been hurriedly called together, and with the payment he received for his help he kept himself in cartridges, golf balls and trout flies for quite a time afterwards.

By no means all the memorable local characters were male. Living in a disreputable little roadside cottage outside the village of Dervaig there was Peigie Challum, a lonely old soul, always greedy for news and wanting to talk, often simply to hear people speaking. She would wait at her gate for someone to come along, and she would stop them and ask if they would bring her some small item from the village, for which she always had a few pennies ready in her hand. One day a friend returned saying, 'Peigi, what do you think? They are saying some explorer has found the North Pole.' This was meat and drink to Peigi. Her eyes bright with excitement, she observed 'Well, well! Fancy that! He'll be aal right now for firewood!'

One lady with a rather interesting nickname was Betsy Gocgoc. This word is associated with the Gaelic *gocaman*, someone always peering round or on watch, like the *gocaman* on the ramparts of Kisimul Castle, Castlebay, who after a trumpet blast would announce, 'MacNeill of Barra has dined; let other princes of the world now dine.' Another lady was called Kate Sklate, and there was Katie Crupach who ran a croft on her own. Molly was another crofter, but male!

A few notables came from a quite different social elevation. Periodically the Justices of the Peace – nearly all gentry

– used to assemble in the Tobermory Court House to pass judgement on local miscreants who had failed to dodge the police. One of the Justices was a most dignified laird who drove his own carriage and pair of fine horses which were put up in the Mishnish Hotel stables while business was being conducted. On one particular day the stable lads gave the horses a big feed of dried peas. When the gentleman with his wife beside him started on his journey home, the exercise brought about a resounding and embarrassing response from the horses which was appreciated by an unusually large crowd lining the streets.

My Uncles – The MacDougalls of Haunn

The MacDougalls of Haunn lived in Treshnish, a remote corner of north west Mull above the coastal cliffs (which featured prominently in the film, *The Eye of the Needle*). They inhabited stout little cottages built long ago with some good ground nearby. There were two families of which Malcolm – Callum Alasdair – was the doyen. He had lived and worked there with his brother Charles from their boyhood, but Charles died young. The two brothers had married two sisters, my Aunts Catherine and Lily.

Lobster fishers, they worked their boat before the days of the auxiliary engine, pulling at the long heavy sweeps (or oars), or putting up a short mast and sail when the wind was favourable. Callum Alasdair was a tall, powerful Hebridean, his language the Gaelic, his English hesitant. In his late 80s and into his early 90s he thought nothing of walking the fifteen miles to Tobermory, leaving home early in the morning and returning in the evening, calling in at Dervaig and at our home in the passing. He lived to be 100.

However, it is about one of his sons, Alick Ban ('Fair'), I'd like to speak, for I knew him well in later years when he

Alick (Ban) Macdougall, the last of the MacDougalls of Haunn, at the lobster fishing. This picture was taken in the mid 1950s.

was living on his own in a tiny cottage beside a sheltered inlet on Quinish estate. He continued lobster fishing as a profitable exercise along the reefs and rocky coast around Caliach. So famous was the quality of the Mull lobsters, he had a firm order from no less than the Cunard Line to send his produce for use on the luxury *Queens*. He would intercept the Staffa and Iona cruise ship as she rounded the north of Mull and hand up his lobsters which were conveyed to Oban, then south by the night train, and were at their destination next day. He was known as the 'Rubber Man' on account of his strength and endurance. He was a mine of information, not only about the ways of the sea, but folklore and Gaelic music. Unfortunately most of this died with him.

He told me many stories of his experiences. Early in the Great War he had been called up to the Navy, serving on the battle cruiser, the *HMS. Invincible*, sunk later at Jutland. As a result of some carelessness he fell from the rigging, hit the railings with his thigh and mercifully fell overboard instead of to his death on the deck. The ship had covered two miles before she could be turned, but Alick was found still floating – like so many of his breed he could not swim. The surgeons saved his leg, and although he walked ever after with a severe limp, it never seemed to trouble him.

He had a hair-raising experience during World War II

which he related to me one day. 'This particular morning,' he said, 'as I came out of the house about six o'clock to get my gear ready for a run over to Caliach, I saw a mine coming floating in with the tide, not fifty yards from the shore. Well, I knew that if that touched the rocks it would be the end of my boat and gear, even the house and myself if I didn't clear out. But I had an idea. I picked up a length of rope and a piece of iron ballast that was lying about, lashed the rope round it and put it in the stern of the wee dinghy I kept for going out to my boat. I took up the oars and backed her gently out to the mine. Oh, I knew fine what a mine was like. I moved to the stern and got a grip at the bottom of a horn and managed to turn the whole thing until I saw a ringbolt. I reached back for the rope and passed it through the ringbolt, gently pushed the mine away and dropped the iron ballast overboard for an anchor. Then I pulled back in, had my breakfast and walked the three miles into Dervaig and phoned the Mine Disposal people. Man, they were quick! I was hardly back than they were out making the mine safe. I wouldn't like their job! I was away up the hill behind a rock with my hands over my ears until they waved that all was safe!'

The Treshnish Islands lie off the north-west coast of Mull and Alick knew every rock, reef and tide-rip there. On Lunga, one of the islands, there are two ruined dwellings where fishermen used to shelter when cut off by the weather, or simply to save doing the return trip of three miles across to the mainland of Mull. They would even plant a few rows of potatoes. The islands have always been a sanctuary for birds. The MacDougalls and others used to make a seasonal collection of eggs and young puffins (in Gaelic *seumas ruadh*, or Red Jimmy) which were salted down in barrels. They were a tasty dish, with a flavour rather like beef.

On the west coast of Lunga, cut off by chasms, is a triangle of cliffs, where the rollers from the open Atlantic break and surge 100ft below. It is called Dun Cruit, the Harp Rock, because of its resemblance to a Celtic harp when seen from certain angles. The summit is covered by a deep layer of earth and grass riddled with the nest burrows of puffins. In days gone by fishermen used to carry the mast of their skiff up to the rock, use it to bridge the 15ft gap, and shin out along it with net bags suspended from their shoulders. These they filled with the delicious young puffins and eggs. As far as Alick knew, only one man had ever been lost when he slipped off the precarious pole to his death far below.

I once asked Alick what had been his most dangerous experience. After some thought he told me. 'It was this time John (his brother) and me were late in coming back from the Treshnish Islands. Well, we knew there was a storm coming up, and it came on us after we had started on our way home. The waves got up with the wind, but we decided to risk it. We couldn't really turn back anyway. So I took the tiller and John held the throttle, and whenever a wave kicked up the stern he slackened off or the propeller would be off her, then he opened up again when it bit. We had to keep her going flat out or we would have been swamped, for the waves were coming from dead astern. The engine got red hot – you could see it glowing. Oh, but we were lucky! We were hardly through the tide-rip off Caliach Point and into the shelter of the land when a cylinder blew up! A piston smashed through the crankcase, but she kept hammering on with the one cylinder until we were just a few hundred yards off our moorings, when it went solid! We took her in with the sweeps.'

Alick was a man of the oars and the sails and the ropes. He never trusted 'those newfangled engines'. To reduce speed he would always 'slacken off' the throttle, as if it were a rope. Another time he was out with John setting lobster creels just a few hundred yards out from the cliffs south of Caliach. It was fairly rough and the wind was on-shore when the engine suddenly stopped. John knew something about engines, and after a quick check he found a stripped pinion in the magneto. By this time they were being carried close in towards the black rocks under the cliff, so John tried a desperate remedy. Cutting off a length of thick tarred twine he asked Alick to turn the engine over by hand as he fed it into the magneto gearing. By a marvellous stroke of luck this worked! He told Alick to turn the engine over hard to start her up – and away she went! 'In fact,' said Alick, 'It was running so good we just left it at that until we got it repaired a fortnight later.'

The lobster creel has changed little in design since my uncles made them nearly a hundred years ago except that the modern one has nylon cordage and manufactured components. It seems no more successful! The creel consists simply of a flat oblong base with a flat stone or weight lashed to it, covered with net stretched over hoops usually of hazel. A funnel entrance at each end gives a no-return way in for the lobster. The more noisome the bait, the more it attracts the lobsters, as the pailful kept under the stern thwart of the boat will testify.

CHAPTER 4

Schooldays

IN OUR SCHOOL AT TOBERMORY simplicity verged on austerity. We sat at old wooden desks, with benches in the lower classes, bearing the initials of past generations, hacked into the wood by their clasp knives. In the more advanced classes stained brass inkwells were fitted and filled with a gooey mixture alleged to be ink which lent itself to pranks, such as flicking a folded strip of inky paper at some unsuspecting target by means of a loose elastic from a dismembered golf ball. A very risky practice from the disciplinary angle!

Not that it really mattered much, for we were an untidy

Tobermory School Standards 3 and 4 in 1913/14
The author is seated in the front row, extreme right
Standing left –
J S Levack, Headmaster ('A ragie aul' billie was he'), and Miss Chrissie Campbell,
Teacher.
Standing right –
Cookstie the Janitor ('Whipper-in')

lot by modern standards. Jerseys and short trousers were the usual garb, and occasionally a jacket. In the case of a few boys from poor families, sometimes a plain ragged kilt was worn, handed down from older pupil-members of the family.

Many boys went barefoot from choice during the summer months and their feet became as tough as those of an Impi of Zulus. With a rough road to travel I always stuck to boots. Shoes were sissy things never worn to school. The boots most envied were those of stout leather with masses of tackets. The imprints left by a new pair in a stretch of half-dried mud would be greatly admired. (There is the story of the Highlandman who exclaimed, 'I had to wear my new boots for a week before I could put them on.') But it was when the rare periods of frost and ice occurred that boots came into their own, especially those with half-worn tackets. Selecting a nice smooth stretch of pavement, we could have a real slippery slide going in no time at all, with an impatient queue of boys, waiting their turn. Of course, there were spoilsports who threw salt on the slides or brought in the police.

After all those years I still shake at a providential escape I had along with my two regular friends, Chisholm and Donnie. We were about twelve years old at the time. We went up to the local reservoir which was thickly frozen over. However, a thaw had set in and there were patches of meltwater on the surface, and a few long cracks. Not to be deterred, after some individual gyrations on the ice, one of us would crouch down in turn and be slid along with our hands held by the other two. Every time we crossed over a crack the water spurted up as the edges sagged under our weight, but we careered merrily along ... out from the bank above 12ft of water. During my midday meal at home I described with great glee and in detail how we had enjoyed our activities and couldn't wait to get back. Quietly but firmly my mother forbade us and suggested any other mischief as an alternative.

As far as girls at school are concerned, my faded memory is of high buttoned boots and 'peenies', or pinafores, that covered unidentifiable garments.

I think it was about 1911 or 1912 that J & P Coats presented every school pupil with a stout cardboard-like knapsack in place of our various satchels for carrying books. They stood astonishing abuse and lasted many years. Mine came in useful at times as a fishing bag.

Younger classes used slates and slate pencils. Intense satisfaction could be had by dragging a pencil at an angle across the slate which produced a squeal that set the teacher's teeth on edge. Reluctantly she had to accept the assurance 'Please, Miss, it's a bad pencil'. Pens were supplied (with questionable nibs) free, together with the ink, but we had to purchase all our own jotters and books, except in the cases of pupils whose parents were on Poor Relief.

Heating in the school in winter was provided by a small coal fire, usually out of sight of the pupils, but where the teacher could shiver least. In former times each pupil was expected to bring a peat to the school. There were no conveyances then, to and from school. There was little traffic on the roads. It was all foot-slogging. I had two miles to go each way, but my home was by no means the most distant. Other scholars had to walk up to five miles, although in winter, if their parents could afford it, those children were boarded out with friends in Tobermory, returning home at weekends. A brother and sister lived six miles 'over the hill' beside the Dervaig road. They had transport consisting of one bicycle on which they 'leap-frogged' their way to school, cycling a certain distance and then leaving the cycle to be picked up by the one walking behind. One concession during the dark days of winter was to allow us to pack up half an hour before finishing time. If the teacher forgot, she was reminded by a chorus of 'Please, Miss, the long-distance people'.

There were no school meals. The midday dinner was either a rush home if you lived in the town, or a 'piece' (sandwich) devoured outside in the shelter shed in the school yard. We must have been tough! This was the background of many a pupil who went on to university and the professions. There were plenty of families in humble circumstances who by considerable sacrifice (for grants were few or non-existent) encouraged their sons and daughters through high school, on to university and into the professions. (A typical example is Neil Cameron, who donated £50,000 towards the cost of building the Craignure ferry terminus in the 1960s.)

The subjects taught were headed by the three 'Rs' – reading, writing and arithmetic. Bible study was important, and we had to memorise psalms and recite verses in turn in the class. Something of the greatness of the words and the rhythm of the psalms remained with us all our lives. Facts were instilled into our unwilling minds by mass class repetition, which must have sounded from outside like something from a Buddhist Order at prayers. But they stuck. Judging from the knowledge displayed on such programmes as University Challenge, we 12-14 year-olds had a far better knowledge of the world's physical geography than today's youngsters.

Built into school discipline was corporal punishment and the strap. Let me say at once that, properly applied and deserved, we did not resent this. We all preferred its quick 'get-it-over-with' to wearisome extra homework. What was degrading was being held to ridicule before the class, and unfortunately there was the occasional sadistic teacher who left pupils nervous and lacking in self-confidence. But discipline and learning were predominant.

Our headmaster was John S Levack, and a 'ragie aul' billie was he'. Although feared, severe and prejudiced, he was a fine teacher. He was a bitter opponent of the speaking of the Gaelic, and I remember well his very words, 'Any pupil I hear speak-

Salvage operation of the Spanish Armada ship in the 1920s in Tobermory Bay.
Alongside the Pier lies the *PS Grenadier.*

ing Gaelic within the precincts of the school will be strapped.'
This was most unwise, for many of my schoolmates were bi-
lingual, expressing themselves in the English language with difficulty. Although my father was a fluent Gaelic speaker and
reader, I never picked up more than a few words, for in the
house it was used only to discuss something I wasn't supposed
to hear, and outside I was something of a loner.

The dying out of Gaelic is a sad outcome of the dying out
of an old generation, although television does its share to
revive it and try to keep it alive. Statistically, in 1881 in Mull
there were 3,400 people who spoke both Gaelic and English,
and among the population were 800 who could only speak
Gaelic. By 1981, 100 years later, those numbers were 628 and
nil respectively.

I must tell you how several of Levack's former and disgruntled pupils were able to pull his leg dramatically, although
he never became aware of it. It happened during the 1912 salvage operations to try to retrieve the mythical treasure sunk in
1588 within the Spanish Armada ship known then as the

Florencia, but as proved in more recent research, the *San Juan de Sicilia*, about 400 yards off the present MacBrayne's pier. The wreck and its contents belonged to the Duke of Argyll, on whose behalf an agent was always present to keep watch for any items of interest raised by the salvage pumps from the timbers. During the school summer holidays Mr Levack was appointed to this post, the remuneration for which was doubtless a useful addition to what must have been a meagre salary.

Some of the odd-job men in Tobermory were engaged as deck hands on the salvage ship. One day one of them went on board with a pocketful of frogs. As Levack was standing by the screens watching the outflow from the powerful pumps, this former pupil slipped the frogs into the flow. Just imagine the dominic's excitement when he saw frogs swimming past on the screen, sucked, it seemed, from their environment under ten fathoms of salt water in Tobermory Bay! He wrote to a number of learned publications, and quite a discussion ensued!

As for time out of school, youngsters created their own games; they had the sea, the hills and the countryside to exploit which gave them healthy pastimes. Crime would be a broken window, football in the streets, poaching rabbits, harmless pranks, although there was always the looming presence of the constable on the beat who sometimes hauled an erring youngster up a close, gave him a cuff on the ear and the warning 'I'll tell your father'. This cowed the culprit most effectively, for he knew what to expect if a complaint reached his parents.

More serious crime was confined to organised poaching, or a rowdy gathering with a punch-up after the pubs closed and the drinkers had been ejected. But for women, the dark, ill-lit streets were as safe at night as on a summer day.

Holidays

The early years of this century were the great days for Rothesay, Dunoon and the Clyde resorts, the sea crowded with competing passenger steamers. The Glasgow Fair was the holiday of the year. This was the time when our bank office at Rothesay had to use baskets to store the cash poured in by ships' pursers, to be sorted and checked once the doors were closed at the end of the day. We in Mull had neither the cash nor the facilities to enjoy such seaside attractions. Our holidays were spent with friends or relatives.

Within our household we could have only one or two outings in the year, for either my father or mother was obliged to remain to supervise the running of Achafraoch House. When we did manage to get away, we hired John Maclean's carriage and pair and were driven over the hill to visit our relatives at Torloisk, Calgary or Penmore. Latterly we travelled in more luxury when an Argyll motor car was substituted for the carriage. The Argyll was one of the most famous cars made in Scotland, embodying a design in advance of its time.

I remember the steep hills where we had to descend from the carriage and walk up in order to give the horses an easier haul. At the summit of the worst of the hills on the Dervaig road a big earthenware trough was installed, filled by a seepage of water to give the horses well-earned refreshment. There were many little springs of lovely cold water at the roadside in the days when wayfarers needed and enjoyed a refreshing drink of water; and beside each spring was a rusty drinking tin suspended on a length of stick.

I would be left with our relatives to enjoy a week or two, helping with the harvest, rounding up sheep or cattle, setting snares for the teeming hordes of rabbits, or at Penmore, walking down to Croig to watch the frenzied activity when coal was unloaded from a puffer tied up alongside the jetty.

A Cellini canon, one of the finds in the wreck of the Spanish galleon, the *San Juan de Sicilia*, wrecked in Tobermory Bay in 1588.
The canon now stands in front of Inveraray Castle, home of the Dukes of Argyll who own the wreck and its contents.

In days long past this was where cattle used to be landed from skiffs which had sailed over from Coll and Tiree, to be driven along the old drove roads through Mull to Grass Point for onward shipment to Oban.

But the really memorable holidays full of adventure were when I was accompanied to my mother's former home in the old fishing village of Portmahomack in Easter Ross. This was an involved journey, in earlier years via the *PS Gael* which sailed in those days from Oban via Tobermory to Kyle of Lochalsh; then by the Highland Railway to Dingwall, there to change to the Thurso train, and so to Fearn station and the last miles by road to 'The Port' as we called it. When the Kyle sailing was discontinued, it was a case of mailboat to Oban, by train on the (now closed) Callander & Oban line of the Caledonian Railway to Dunblane or Stirling, usually changing at Perth, then by Druimochter to Inverness and the north

Those were really great holidays. The magnificent sandy beach came right to the wall on the other side of the road from the house that had been built by my great-grandfather, who had also built the little harbour works and curing shed, all so different from Mull. There were big, fertile fields stretching towards the lighthouse, and the ruins of Balone Castle to explore and search in vain for the secret vaults that hold the treasure of a Norwegian Jarl. There were still a few fishermen who used high-bowed cobbles (locally called co'bles), and hung their nets high on poles for drying and cleaning.

(A dying village between the wars, Portmahomack has blossomed, smartened up with new houses, my grandfather's curing sheds now turned into blocks of modern flats. The open beach looking across the Dornoch Firth to the distant hills of Sutherland is now a popular centre for windsurfing and holidays. The flat coast stretches to Tain, and halfway along, on the offshore sandy flats, there is now a bombing range for aeroplanes from Lossiemouth.)

At home in Mull I created my own amusements, whether playing at battles with homemade materials in the big empty ward I used as a playroom, or fishing my preserves in the river, as we called the burn that held the house in a shining loop. I wonder now if the Tobermory schoolboys of today are as active? Do they still walk up from the town on hot summer days, toss off their clothes and revel uninhibited in the cool refreshing waters of the pool we called 'The Big Ling'? And do the older and more adventurous lads venture into that awesome, dark, deep pool further down we called 'The Ling in the Stabs' – the pool said to be the haunt of a water-horse waiting to drag the unwary down under its still surface? I don't think we would have been fooled, for a water-horse is easily recognised by its unnaturally short ears as it grazes along the bank, inviting people, especially young maidens, to jump on for a short gallop which ends finally deep in the pool.

My schoolmates used to fish far up the river past our house, leaving beaten tracks along the banks among the heather and bracken. All such traces were absent the last time I revisited my old haunts.

Do boys still build *bothacks* (little bothies) to celebrate the Easter holidays? This was an old tradition, although as boys we didn't know that. It comes down from the days when the womenfolk and youngsters moved in the late spring from the townships up to the hill shielings, taking the livestock with them, which allowed the menfolk to prepare the ground for crops in the days before the land was walled and fenced. In the shielings, while the livestock grazed on the hill grass, the people lived in rude *bothans* in something of a holiday spirit. You will still see traces of these when walking the hills.

The procedure for constructing our *bothacks* was this. We gathered in secret groups and built rude little shelters made from any materials we could find, beg or borrow. We would meet in it on Good Friday and enjoy gorging ourselves on lemonade and fancy cakes we bought from Allan Dally's van with the pennies we had been saving from our meagre weekly allowances.

I have never forgotten one such *bothack* which Donnie, Chisholm and I built with much toil and preparation in a convenient angle of the quarry behind the house. My father did not miss the small roll of wire netting we proposed to spread over the roof to carry a thatch of heather, but we needed half a dozen rafters. Most conveniently, a load of those had been delivered at the gate of Dougie MacQuarrie's nearby croft, so we collected a few and duly set them up. Just as we had almost completed the structure with its smooth turf walls and even a length of drainpipe erected as a chimney over a stone fireplace, Dougie met us and indicated he was short of the exact number of stobs we had requisitioned, and they were to be returned forthwith! Or else! Within our de-roofed walls we still managed to celebrate Good Friday in the customary fashion.

We had intricate games such as marbles, and of course the perennial football, for which we had no playing field, and we trundled 'reelers', hoops, girrs, or whatever – some kind of iron hoop pushed and guided by the crook on a long iron rod. I had a beauty, the thin iron rim of some small wheel from a discarded vehicle. The name 'reeler' arose from the 'reeling' sound made by the contraption in motion.

The boys from 'down the town' had fun messing about in boats, and their location for swimming was below the Lighthouse road, at Port-a'-Choit, a short distance north of MacBrayne's pier.

Reading Matter

Reading was a fine way of passing the time during the long, dreary winter months. For the distaff side of the house there was the *People's Friend* and *My Weekly* and the occasional magazine. There were no Sunday papers. They did not appear until the 1930s, when the small ferry boat at Grass Point began to bring them in from Oban. My father went every day on his beloved bicycle to collect his copy of *The Scotsman* (a day late) from Hughie Cameron's newspaper shop, at the back of which there was a mysterious machine for bottling aerated waters. The glass bottles were sealed by a glass ball housed inside the neck that we prized very much for our games of marbles, even if we had to smash a bottle to secure the marble.

My most vivid recollection is of the magazines and week-lies for boys, such as the *Magnet* and the *Gem* and the *Union Jack*, featuring exciting stories of inter-school rivalries, and the adventures and successful cases of Sexton Blake, that brilliant detective who outshone even the great Sherlock Holmes. We used to exchange magazines, thus getting an even greater variety of excitement. The grammar and quality of writing of those publications for juveniles was excellent. I now regard these 'trash of books', as my disapproving parents called them, as unconscious lessons in English composition and grammar for which there is no equal today. The popularity of some of the fictional characters persists – Flashman, the bully of *Tom Brown's Schooldays*, lives on as a despicable hero in the *Flashman* books of George McDonald Fraser.

As we grew older we devoured the books of Ballantyne, Henty, Conan Doyle, 'Sapper', Walsh, Gunn and many others.

CHAPTER 5

Fishing for Profit and Pleasure

LET ME TELL YOU about some of my experiences of sharing the rich harvest of the sea in the Sound of Mull during the 1920s and earlier.

Our favourite haunt was the reef known as the Stirks, off Tobermory Bay. With three or four of us in the boat, we rowed out to the location. We set a stout plank across the boat near the stern where two of us sat, facing aft, each with two long, light, bamboo rods spread fanwise across the stern, the butts jammed under the plank. On short lines, hooks with scraps of white feathers tied on were trailed behind the boat as it was rowed gently round the reef. We often found ourselves in the middle of a shoal of mackerel, saithe or lythe, and got a fish on every hook. We would frantically pull them in, clear them off the hooks and simply toss them into the boat behind us – then out with the lines again. We could often count on taking 200-300 fish in an evening, to be divided into lots and shared out amongst people we knew.

Sometimes we hooked one of those big coalfish we called *piocach* which was too heavy to be hauled in, whereupon we simply dropped the floating rod over the side and picked it up next time round, with the fish played out by fighting the rod. They made rather coarse eating. One day an enthusiastic visitor hired a boat to try his luck. Sure enough, he was enjoying some good sport when he hooked one of those big *piocach*. Having heard of our method of playing the fish, and before the boatman could stop him, he dropped his nice greenheart rod overboard – and watched with horror as it sank deep down into the waving beds of kelp far below.

The author departing on a fishing trip in 1920

My father loved sea fishing off the rocky coast. His favourite spot, Penalbranach, lay about four miles distant from home by moorland paths, which meant his sea-fishing outings were confined to a few occasions only. When I was old enough I accompanied him, but when we got there I preferred pottering along the unaccustomed shore, investigating floatsam and jetsam, and scaring the wits out of the inhabitants of rock pools. We were once cut off by the tide on a rocky outcrop and my father had to hoist me on his back and wade waist-deep to safety. He used a rod like a trimmed pine tree with something like a hawser supporting a hefty lead weight, and a hook embedded in soft crab kept in place by a winding of sheep's wool picked up as we went along. His prey were those stumpy big-scaled shell-crushing *creagag* – rockfish or green wrasse – that lived deep down in the kelp beds under the rocks; when one was hooked, my father had to react instantly or it would wind itself round the rubbery stems and be lost.

In the Sound of Mull there was no lack of fish to be found, always sought by locals 'for the pot'. Lobster fishing was, of course, a very old practice around Mull's rocky coasts, and there was stake netting for salmon in certain rented sections of the coast.

Until the beginning of the 20th century a simple and effective salmon trap was in operation at the mouths of rivers and estuaries in Mull and elsewhere. The trap consisted of a level winding drystone dyke built across the river mouth from shore to shore at low tide. At high water it becomes deeply submerged and salmon and seatrout drift inshore across it, attracted by the richly oxygenated fresh water from the river. As the tide recedes and the dyke becomes uncovered, fish are left stranded and can be simply picked up. An excellent example is to be seen across a branch of the estuary of the River Bellart at Dervaig, which was regularly repaired and preserved by one of the old Dervaig families and was still in use early in the 20th century. I was told that the record haul for a single tide was sixty salmon! As there was no question of commercialism, the Dervaig people fed well on salmon for a fortnight after. The boundaries of most estates ended at the high water mark, so this kind of fish trapping was outwith the jurisdiction of the lairds, much to their infuriation.

At the mouth of the river we used to enjoy casting and spinning for seatrout, with the chance of a salmon, at high tide. My friend Alick Ban once confessed to me that late one evening, when the tide was right and no-one was about, he experimented by stretching a net across the narrow channel leading into a small bay at Croig, just to see if it was visited by salmon. Returning at daybreak and starting to pull in the net, he was embarrassed by his catch, which, of course, he could not sell. The disposal of so many fish was a problem,

Fishergirls at Tobermory Pier in 1920. These girls followed the herring fishing fleet wherever there were jobs gutting and barrelling the fish.

Drifters – herring fishing boats – at Tobermory Pier in 1920

and for weeks afterwards he was baiting his lobster creels with salmon.

In the late 18th century Tobermory had been selected for development as a fishing port. Although its suitability for fish landings could never compete with mainland ports such as Oban and Mallaig, its excellent anchorage provided safe haven for all kinds of vessels, and fishing boats used to anchor by the dozen in Tobermory Bay in really stormy weather. They ranged from big Iceland trawlers to the small liners and drifters, and registrations varied from BCK (Buckie), SY (Stornoway) to FD (Fleetwood). The crews used to come ashore for a refreshment at the local hotel bars, where you would hear a great variety of dialects. In order to raise the necessary spending money, they would sell a few prime fish along at the Old Pier. Once as I was on my way home from school, I decided to give my parents a treat, and for a sixpence (2¹/₂p) I was given a cod, full of roe, that must have weighed six pounds. I toddled home with the cod's tail trailing on the road behind me. How I happened to have the munificent sum of sixpence in my pocket remains a complete mystery.

Fresh Water Fishing

Sitting in my armchair, with my battered home-made stick at my side, I can shut my eyes and be transported back to the days of my youth. I can see that big, flat, revolving pancake of foam at the Falls Pool, under which the huge strange trout appeared after floodwaters, greedily grabbing the worm I dropped at the limit of reach of my cranky old rod; or in later years, dropping a dainty fly on the once-forbidden lochs to entice the wary, red-spotted trout.

I am just a very ordinary angler as far as catching fish is concerned, but I do admit to having a large amount of knowledge about their habits and habitats, ever since those long summer days spent along the river bank in Mull – just watching.

Our home lay within a loop of a substantial hill burn we called The River, a comfortable two miles from Tobermory up the quiet dusty road leading over to the west side of the island. The river fascinated me ever since the day I fell in during a mini-spate when reaching for a bunch of globe flowers. I was probably three years old at the time. Fortunately I landed upright in an eddy close to the low bank and was able to drag myself out and return to the house where I left a trail of water and muddy footprints across the immaculate linoleum. The only other time I fell in was many years later when I was reliving my childhood by dropping an experimental worm into some familiar corner. As I leaned casually on a mossy stump, it slowly gave way. I over-balanced gently and wetly on my back. By good luck I was unobserved, so I managed to preserve my dignity.

When my father realised my fishing ambitions, he cut a long thin branch from a willow tree, trimmed it, and tied on a length of thin line that could be bought in those days for one penny, with hook 'to gut' at two for a penny. This was long before the days of graded nylon available in unlimited lengths such as we have today. The brittle gut was lashed firmly to the hook. It had to be thoroughly soaked before any knots could be tied, otherwise it broke. It came in lengths of about 12" which had to be joined up to make a fly cast. Most flies were 'to gut', although eyed flies were always available.

Having persuaded someone to impale a protesting worm on the hook, I trotted proudly to the bank, thrilled to the core. Of course I caught nothing, which was not surprising; firstly, the worm dropped no more than two feet from the bank; then I hadn't the faintest idea where the trout lay; and finally, fast and still water were all the same to me.

As it was many years before I could afford the tackle and equipment for which I sighed, I had to improvise. My brother and sister were much older than me, and heading for university and training college respectively in Edinburgh. In those days bursaries and grants were negligible, although the days were past when a student carried with him enough oatmeal and salt herring to last out the term! In our cash-strapped household I was financially the odd man out; not that I grudged them their opportunities, it was just unfortunate. Or was it? I had the compensation of living so much longer at home with kindly and indulgent parents. But it wasn't until my twenties, before I was transferred to the head office of the bank where I started my life's work, that I was at last able to scrape together a few shillings from my meagre salary and afford a few essentials, like fishing tackle.

In my early schooldays I was able to replace the most tattered of my hooks and lines by collecting and selling bottles at one penny each to a sometimes reluctant grocer. I had a weekly allowance from my father of a penny or two, which was augmented if I could truthfully report some successful school work – and I always stuck to the truth in spite of the temptation! And there was also the odd coin from a visiting relative.

I was bitten, not by the fish, but with a craze to fish that carried me from humble beginnings to the end of a long active life of angling. Using a longer branch and growing experience I caught my first trout, an unwary 5" fish that should have known better. Still too scared of wriggly worms and biting trout, I dragged my catch to the nearest adult, who after expressing his congratulations and admiring my catch with assumed amazement, unhooked it for me and impaled a fresh worm.

It was by sympathetic instinct I began to tap my catches on the head to end their sad flapping, or, handling an under sized fish carefully with moistened hands (to avoid drying and damaging the scales), slip it back into the water none the worse.

My father unearthed a real greenheart rod, cranky, brittle, all of 8ft long, and with a reel that sometimes worked. This opened up new horizons for me. Of course, the rod broke sometimes. There was the sad occasion when I hooked one of those big trout in a small pool where it had no business to be. That was in the Fence Pool (all my pools had a name). I struck and lifted as usual, to see a mighty trout of, I am sure, a pound in weight hoisted to the surface, to the accompaniment of a double crack as my rod snapped in two places. Of course the trout vanished in a cloud of spray, nor could I entice it back later. My father was an expert at splicing and he taught me how to do so with maximum neatness. During my golfing years I broke the wooden shaft of my favourite putter, and I spliced it, but instead of using the customary tarred thread I used nylon, making a far lighter, neater, stronger and less conspicuous job.

A New Rod

The tackle I used when a boy was crude, and to begin with I had the cranky old spliced rod. And yet I'm sure I caught as many burn trout then as I can do now with my 9ft Hardy rod that can flick a fly for 22 yards just where I want it and is better than the outfits we used to envy in the hands of the gentry. The 12" lengths of cat gut of unreliable quality had to be soaked before knotting and again before we began to cast.

My real angling years, the end of the 'chuck it and chance it' days, began in 1916, when I was twelve. My Uncle Hugh was head foreman in the Heavy Ship Repairs section of the great John Brown's shipyard on the Clyde. He always spent a holiday with us at the Glasgow Fair. This time, under wartime pressure, Uncle Hugh could snatch only a few days. It was just after the battle of Jutland, and he described how *HMS Lion*, after a mauling, was brought to the shipyard for repairs in a near sinking condition, with holes you could drive a horse and cart through!

When Uncle Hugh arrived in Mull – what joy! – he presented me with a handsome, brand-new, 11ft greenheart rod, with reel and line complete, and a small selection of flies. What a gift! He could cast a useful fly, so we resorted to the long, quiet, deep reaches of the river among the peat bogs where a worm was never a success. The fascination of how he could cast and present the flies, the eruption of a few river trout and the landing of them on what seemed to me the flimsiest of tackle, had me hooked in a new dimension. Old habits died hard, and for a few years I slung a worm into corners hitherto inaccessible; but that became kids' stuff. The fly became increasingly and finally the way to fish. And so it went on until I acquired even more selective equipment.

The rest of my tackle was completely makeshift. On my feet I wore a pair of big army boots discarded by my brother. For a landing net, I had such difficulty in selecting the exact design that I decided to make my own, which I used all my fishing life. I required a edge to the net that was neither too square nor too round; something that would be stout enough to cut or slip through under a weeded trout. I took a length of stout fence wire, bent it into the generous oval size I wished and fixed on an extra deep net. This was spliced to a long handle of lightweight wood (handy, too, as a wading staff), and I slung the contraption over my shoulder with a clip-on dog lead for quick release! I made my own fly box. 'An ill-favoured thing, sir, but my own.' The first flies I bought could be had for as little as tuppence each; threepence was normal. They were not as neatly tied as modern flies, but freely accepted by the unsophisticated island trout. Of course, I always carried my pocket knife of good old-fashioned steel I kept sharpened to a razor edge, I and wore a wide-brimmed hat, useful both for shading the eyes from glare and as a handy place round which to wind a cast.

The Ways of a Trout

From my earliest days, with my enthusiasm centred on the river where I sailed my home-made boats and bombarded the hostile flotilla of ducks with shells made from soft peat, it was natural that I'd get to know a great deal about those denizens of the deep – the trout; and with less enthusiasm, the eels. When the river was low during the rainless weeks of early summer that ended inevitably with the Glasgow Fair floods, I used to wade along the shallows, turning over stones with an old spade, learning where the fish were likely to be found and noting every rock and obstruction that could threaten the natural movement of my bait under fishing conditions.

The few really big strangers that appeared in 'my' river after a flood seemed to congregate in the Falls Pool. They were trout in rather poor condition; there was not enough food in the river to feed them. The laird was known to hold the theory that they were seatrout, exhausted after ascending the falls and cataracts from the sea three miles distant. I knew better, for by the law of averages, if a seatrout passed along my beats, I must catch one, and this never happened. No, those were big trout adventuring over the overflow from the chain of little lochs a couple of miles up the river, settling down in the Falls Pool as the only suitable habitat, and lacking floodwaters, unable to return.

Author's son and daughter after floods on the Tobermory River at the 'Falls Pool', 'haunt of the giant trout', in 1948.

The Falls Pool was naturally my special preserve. A cataract poured down steeply across one side of the pool, leaving a great revolving circle of pure white foam on the other side. Under this the big fish lay in wait for the insects that dropped from the overhanging swaying branches of hazel bushes, where in late autumn I swung round precariously – as on a windjammer, one hand for myself, the other reaching out for those delicious brown hazel nuts, the best of which were always out of reach, twenty feet above the foam below. The nuts could be split open by a cunning flip of my pocket knife, thus avoiding dental breakages. (All my life I carried a really sharp pocket knife, indispensable for angling and much more, including surreptitious erasing of wrong figures in bank books, a practice frowned upon by my superiors, although the knife was much in demand by my bank colleagues in every branch in which I served.)

I remember one hot day sitting on the bank of the Bridge Pool with my feet on a partly submerged rock under which a 6" trout had scurried at my approach. Presently I felt a slight vibration under my feet, and out popped the head of an eel holding the trout across its jaws. I had my spade with me, and as it emerged, I drove the edge of the spade down, which missed the eel but caused it to draw back in a hurry and release the trout, which shot away apparently unharmed. I understood then how the occasional trout I caught had the triangular mark of an eel's jaws on its side. I always disliked eels, even if I respected their fascinating life story. If they took a worm, they bolted it so far down and turned line and gut into such a writhing tangle that I had to kill them to retrieve the valuable hook and avoid giving them inevitable suffering. Often if you allowed the worm to drift deeply in the slow current of a pool, there came the unmistakable take of an eel. I soon learned to keep to faster water.

I sometimes tried my hand at 'guddling', which consists of lying on the bank with sleeve tucked up to the shoulder, gently inserting the fingers under a rock until they are under an unsuspecting trout, then trying to flip it out. I soon stopped doing this when I tried it on what was, in fact, an eel! Luckily I escaped injury!

The Fence Pool was a useful little pool, cut deeply into

the peaty bank, with a smooth gravelly bottom. With great caution I would move my head into the thick heather above the water and gently part the stems, and this gave me a clear view of the underwater world, where I could watch the habits of a small queue of trout. I experimented by shouting at them, and dispelled the admonition of 'No talking when fishing', for they ignored this airborne noise. But let me thump my toes on the ground behind me and every fish became alert, and the slightest movement of my head against the skyline sent them scurrying into cover, from which they emerged cautiously five minutes later.

It was amusing to watch the pecking order below. The queue of fish was poised exactly in the dead water between the main current and the return eddy, strategically sited to inspect with the least effort any promising item carried past. Even in a fast current you find patches of dead water around a submerged rock. The queue was in order of size. The leader, lord of the pool and perhaps 8" or 9" in length, was at the head, with first claim, followed by two or three others, investigating the leader's discards. The poor wee fish at the end had to keep dashing around to keep its place hoping for some tit-bit missed by the others. When the leader moved out to investigate something really interesting, the rest moved one fish up, until the big fellow returned and chivvied his temporary successor until the queue moved one fish back.

From all those hours of watching I learned a lot that helped me in years to come, both with the fly and later when I tackled the salmon: it likes to poise itself as much as possible in fast water, but with a different urge – not to feed, but to rejoice in the more richly oxygenated quality of broken water, for they do not feed in fresh water. When they take a fly or lure it is out of curiosity, a vague memory of their salt water feeding days, or sheer irritation.

When occasonally school colleagues came poaching on

my preserves, even under low water conditions and thanks to my local knowledge, much to their disgust I could always pick up a trout, so they would move away down to the deep pool of The Linn, to bathe in the sluggish water where nothing but the fly could tempt the fish. The last time I visited my river – 85 years after those first days – there were no longer paths worn through the scrub along the banks by youngsters, for their enthusiasm is now channelled into the less simple pursuits of modern sophistication.

Mull's rivers are short and depend on floodwaters to allow the ascent of seatrout and salmon. They were, of course, strictly preserved by the estates. However, there were a few where fishing for trout was not discouraged by the landowners; and in any case, nearly all the lesser burns have their own stock of brown trout, so there was fishing for everyone. Our modest number of anglers in Tobermory was lucky in this respect, for we fished with some security on the banks of the Mishnish Lochs, always fishing fair, and retiring as unobserved as possible, if a gamekeeper appeared on the skyline or when the laird himself came rowing along with his boatman at the oars. We could have brazened it out with authority if accosted, for the only way we could have been expelled was either by fishing using illegal methods or being interdicted, i.e. legally excluded, from that part of the estate.

A great change has taken place in the intervening years. Lochs that once were taboo are now rented to Angling Associations such as the Tobermory Angling Club, and boats are available where once there were none.

Exploring Further Afield, Especially for Fish

Limited at first by my age and tackle to the river banks beside our house, my horizon gradually expanded with improving gear and experience. Even fuller mobility came when I was allowed to use my father's bicycle, although with great care, for it was a machine of which he was very proud.

For some time my beats were confined to the Falls Pool up the river, and to the rougher and less productive stretch downstream to the Linn, that natural swimming pool in the summer months. Below the Linn was the winding stretch of sluggish deeps where Uncle Hugh showed me how to cast a fly. This ended at a stone barrier, a wide basaltic dyke near the Druid Stones, and below that was a great mysterious pool at the head of the cataracts that led down to the town and the sea, a portion of the river in which I had no interest. Even now, I can still visualise in detail every corner into which I could drop a worm and expect a response.

As the years went on I extended my activities far above the Falls Pool to the point where the river forked. One branch wandered through the peat bogs from the outflow of Loch Pellac; not a very productive length, but it was conveniently close to the main road. The other branch which supplied the town's reservoir (now abandoned in favour of the three lochs) was worth a visit in itself for its greedy wee trout. Above it the burn, now much reduced in volume, wandered in a strange unknown country, and was tenanted by a race of not very large and unhandsome trout in its peaty waters. Following it, you arrived at last at the low cliffs of what is known as the Crater Hill, under which it disappeared, doubt-less an underground flow from the Crater Loch that lay above, deep within the perimeter of the crater. This is one of the lesser volcanoes that broke through the earlier lava sheets towards the end of the Tertiary period.

A tiny overflow ran from the lower end of the Crater Loch down to Loch Meadhoin, crossing the main road beside the ruined house of the former keeper, beside which I pitched my little green tent when I came back on holiday in later years. It was ocupied finally by a family closely related to Jimmy Black, the gamekeeper. From earliest schooldays I was very friendly with the son of the house, whose status allowed us some legitimate latitude and less attention, especially on the Top and Middle lochs, and on a certain burn which provided a nice dish of seatrout during times of flood. In later years his solitary duties as a roadman had made him a knowledgeable student of wildlife, as well as a good teller of local lore, all of which he shared with me at his fireside. He was skilled in the use of rod and gun in a gentlemanly manner, for he fished and shot purely for the pot. It was during this period that I held for two or three years the (unofficial) record of a two-and-a-half pound trout, caught when casting from the dark headland on the south side of Loch Carnan nan Amais on my favourite fly, the silver Butcher, size twelve, fished on the tail of the cast. He netted it for me after I had guided it for 40 yards round the steep rocky bank.

I always felt there was a strange atmosphere of loneliness and something else in the part of the moorland below the crags of Crater Hill that left me vaguely uneasy. The sun never seemed to shine as brightly. This centred on three or four rings of stones that marked the sites of ancient human habitations. Round them the heather grew long and rank, as if fighting vainly to obliterate them. Inside each ring coarse grass was growing with a centre patch of nettles, which you will always find where man has been. Who were those mysterious people who lived in such an inhospitable place, without a single scrap of potentially arable land near them? I always passed by quickly and uneasily; for might this not have had something to do with the Little Folk?

The chain of three lochs locally called the Mishnish Lochs that lay further up-river conveniently skirting the main road now became my main centre of activities. At first, with my new long-casting rod, I could sling a big soft worm even well into the prevailing westerly winds from my special corners, but it was easier said than done, catching some of those fabulous trout. The lowest of the lochs is Loch Pellac, the Loch of the Monster, from which emerges the branch of the river I have mentioned. I would describe some of the trout as large, but certainly not monsters! The middle loch is Loch Meadhoin, Middle Loch, which was a favourite of mine, both from bank and boat. Loch Carnan nan Amais, the Top Loch, has a very interesting name. *Carnan* is a small heap of stones and *Amais* is translated as a meeting place.

At the west end of the loch, exactly at the fourth milestone which is the halfway point between Tobermory and Dervaig, and between it and the shore of the loch, there are tiny heaps of stones, now mostly covered up by coarse heather, bracken and road detritus. These are said to mark the resting point of funeral parties travelling the eight miles of road between Tobermory and Kilmore cemetery at Dervaig. On departing the spot, each mourner was expected to lay a stone, so small cairns were formed. (From the earliest times, stones and pebbles seem to have been associated with the dead, dating from ancient times when stones were heaped on a grave to keep off wild animals.) This point of the road, too, marks the end of the length of comparatively level road before it drops steeply down to Loch Torr and rises again even more steeply at Achnadrish to the watershed high above Dervaig. What would be more natural than that travellers would all rest and meet here by the little cairns?

At the head of Loch Pellac there were overhanging peaty banks below which lay flooded trenches of old peat cuttings, covered when the level of the loch was raised by building a dam across the narrow outflow over a century ago (to ensure the flow of water for the town distillery). In the evening big fish would drift in to feed on insects dropping from the heathery fringe above. Here one had to tread softly to avoid an earth tremor that would put down the fish. I would stand far back, and with a long cast let the flies drop naturally over the edge.

These lochs were then strictly private, and I was obliged to keep a watchful eye on the skyline for John Fraser, the be-whiskered Aros gamekeeper, and Jimmy Black, his Erray counterpart. How often have I waited impatiently among the bushes and long bracken until it was safe. Mind you, with hindsight, I do believe my activities, and those of the one or two other local anglers, were well enough known to them, but they knew we fished fair.

I found that the Crater Loch carried a good stock of trout, put in long, long before. However, in its stony inhospitable water the fish would have to work harder to find food, so they were darker and less plump. This loch is notable for the occasion when I was fishing it in company with a local friend who was the respected minister of one of Glasgow's churches. Teetering out on some precarious stones to reach a rising trout he slipped and landed knee-deep in the water. Even from across the other side I heard with admiration and a new respect the expletives he addressed to all and sundry!

A couple of miles beyond the three lochs is Loch Torr, taking its name from the Torr, or little isolated hill, above the road and overlooking the loch. This is an artificial loch, created 100 years ago by the building of a 15ft dam in the narrow neck of the glen just beyond the confluence of two burns. The length of the Mingary burn flowing out of it was cleared of all obstructions, allowing salmon and seatrout to ascend from the sea. Very few salmon were ever caught; the best I have ever heard of was a twelve-pounder in the early days of

Loch Torr – The author at dusk, the seatrout coming in, in 1972

the loch. However, seatrout come readily to the fly, a thrilling alternative to the native brown trout. The Mingary burn is also an excellent place for catching seatrout on the worm when they are coming up in flood waters! I found that Loch Torr was a delight to fish, either off the east bank (the west bank is rough and afforested) or better still in the boat, once I had learned the location of the lines of the submerged beds of the burns frequented by the fish and the best drifts.

The growing dearth of freshwater mussels in Scottish rivers (it is now an offence to kill them) reminds me that a local friend told me that many years ago he found mussels in the Caoltri burn, one of the two entering Loch Torr. He opened and examined a few and discovered one or two small pearls, the best of them worth no more than £5 when he found a buyer.

The Loch of the Stranger is a strange little loch, immensely deep, in fact a geological freak, as if a long crack had occurred near the edge of a lava escarpment. It was once the special preserve of the estate, and, somewhat unnecessarily, even had a boat on it, a few fragments of which are still lying on the shore. Little rock platforms were built out from the shore where depth allowed, highly convenient for casting. The location of the loch is so well hidden that visiting anglers find it hard to find; fortunately, for its stock of trout would soon be exhausted. My best was a handsome trout of 2lbs.

A climb up the steep heather slope of the hill on the west side of the loch takes you to the divide, and just below, hidden from the right of way that passes along the valley below, is the small Red Loch. This is rarely fished, but, as is usual in Mull's lochs and burns and rivers, it has its stock of trout. Here, beside the edge of the loch, I once almost stepped on the nest of a merganser, the bird sliding into the water like a snake at my approach. How did those remote, originally troutless waters, many with little outflows, come to have trout in them? I can only think that, over the centuries, the eggs of fish have been carried there stuck on the legs of ducks and wading birds, to be dropped into the water, where they hatched and developed.

Now most of these waters are managed by the town Angling Clubs, with membership or day tickets; but all the fun is gone! I used to say that if I saw another angler at the far end of a loch I would pack up in disgust, complaining that the place was becoming too busy! Now the banks are trodden into paths by the feet of anglers, and there are boats available for locals and visitors. Rainbow trout are included in the re-stocking. While they are rewarding for quick growth and size, I much prefer the beauty and lines of the brown trout. Rainbows are rather over-rated, I think. The 'rainbow' markings are an illusion, and I don't like the snub noses and tails that appear to have been half-bitten!

Later I discovered that there are, of course, many more

sophisticated waters in Mull, for instance the salmon river, the Lussa, which runs through the picturesque Strathcoil from the three little lochs in Glen More and down to the sea in Loch Spelve. Although the salmon eluded me, I have picked up the occasional seatrout here. From above the Falls of Lussa at low water in summer I have watched the restless movements of a small salmon and an attendant seatrout, or a small salmon/grilse that occasionally seemed to lose patience, and circle the pool, always returning to its original place beside a submerged rock as it waited for a flood to allow it to surmount the falls and ascend to the lochs two miles distant, lochs I have never fished.

Salmon and seatrout go up the Aros river from Salen Bay and there must be a good stock of them in Loch Frisa during the season, although few are caught. I certainly never saw or touched anything like the 45lb salmon caught in the 1880s

The summit cairn and crater loch of 'S Airde Ben, with Ben More in the distance. Often fished by the author.

and recorded in the estate game book. It was thought that this might be one of a pair (for its twin was seen in the river) heading for the River Awe and Loch Awe but which became disoriented.

I must not forget the fun of fishing for seatrout at the little estuary of the Bellart burn below Dervaig, when a high tide coincided with a heavy flow of fresh water, and the incoming water crept over the salty grassy banks unnoticed until it reached the tops of one's gum boots. Here I joined the youth of the village busy with worm tackle and catching the occasional small seatrout. I would put the fly far out to where I could see the fish moving and pull in a few smaller ones that go under various local names such as finnock. Once I hooked something really big, but what with the clumps of floating seaweed and my awkward stance, I hadn't a hope of landing it.

Angling from a Boat

One day early in the 1920s, three of us were given the privilege of using the Aros estate boat on Loch Pellac. Our total bag was 41 trout from 1½lbs downwards. Dusk was falling and we were about to pack up. I was at the oars, gently edging the boat over to a fitful patch of wind-ruffled water on the otherwise glassy surface. My friend in the stern had set his rod down carelessly with the flies trailing behind on a short line. Suddenly a big trout exploded out of the water, snatched a trailing fly, and before he could grab it, the rod had been jerked overboard. In the increasing dusk all we could do was to take cross bearings. Returning next day with a grapnel normally used for retrieving lost deep-sea lines, we had been searching for an hour when we brought up the tip of the rod in 10ft of water. The line was out right to the end of the backing. As it was being reeled in we saw the flash of a fish deep below, and when the strain came on we found two fighting fish still hooked. They were of over a pound and just under a pound respectively in weight. The third fly was missing, so it was a matter of speculation what size the third trout would have been. Obviously the first fish had roamed round dragging the other flies, which interested fish into taking them. The overnight soaking had ruined the old splitcane rod.

My father brought me up to be careful in boats, and boat safety came home to me during my early years after the experience of two elderly anglers on a day's outing on Loch Frisa. Few boats were then to be seen on the loch. The men were rowing and trolling with their rods over the stern and long lines out. Suddenly, to their utter amazement, a salmon leaped and grabbed one of the small flies; the rod jumped and the tip bent into the water. Now, although salmon and seatrout can ascend easily to the loch and are caught in the outflow river Aros, they are rarely taken on the loch. In their excitement the two men jumped to their feet, the boat tilted, and they overbalanced into the water with the boat upside down beside them. All they could do was to hold on where they could. By a sheer miracle there happened to be another boat from the Salen hotel out on the loch and not so far away, so the occupants saw the accident. Heaving at the oars they arrived just in time to rescue the two men, now exhausted and their grips slipping. By next day they were none the worse, but rods, tackle and all were lost.

The Glengorm boat on Loch Meadhoin was a delight to handle and gradually I learnt all the best drifts and corners to fish. Every year in a little bay I admired the display of creamy waterlilies, now covering about an acre, after a basket of lily roots was sunk in the peaty bottom over 100 years ago. It is a tangle of rubbery roots given a wide berth by anglers. At the corner of the bay stands an ancient birch tree, and I am sure embedded in the bark you will still find the rusted remains of flyhooks hung up and broken off by generations of anglers.

When the wind became just too strong and the boat drifted too fast I used a drogue, or light anchor, consisting of a brick or stone lashed to a thin rope let out and secured midships where I could reach it readily from the oars thwart. This slowed up the boat and kept it broadside to the wind, most suitable for casting. By moving the rope fore and aft along the gunwale I could make the boat swing or zig-zag across an arc of 60 or 80 degrees without touching the oars, thus covering a much greater area of water. I preferred to fish alone in the boat, to move at will, go ashore at will, without anyone near me ... whose careless back-cast could wind his flies around my neck!

Loch Frisa is the largest loch in Mull, over four miles in length by under a mile at its widest. My father and I would walk the five miles to the head of the loch, where we were given the use of the hotel boat. This is an exposed, windy stretch of water, and hard to fish at times without someone at the oars, but it carries a stock of the loveliest multi-spotted trout I have ever seen. On a perfect day we used to count our catch in dozens, with an occasional trout up to a pound weight. 50 to 60 was a common figure for those small red-fleshed beauties that fought like something twice their size.

Over the years I became to be able to tell at a glance not only from which loch a trout had been taken, but the exact spot: deep, rocky, peaty, weedy, for the trout assumed camouflage colouring to match their habitat.

The shores of Loch Frisa are steep, so when rowing or drifting, the boat is best kept parallel to the shore and about 30 or 40 yards off, so that you can see the rocky bottom on one side and deeper water on the other. And the wind! How often have we rowed energetically for two miles down the loch, our lines trolling behind the boat – which is sometimes a very effective method of catching the fish here – depending on the wind to blow us comfortably back home with an occasional touch of the oars, allowing us to cast all the way. But there might come a sudden lull, a change of direction as the wind veered, and we would have to pull our arms off all the way home. By then it would be evening, when the wind usually drops, and once ashore we had to face clouds of voracious midges all the five miles home. It was fine for my father; he was a heavy pipe smoker of black Bogey Roll tobacco, the ominous clouds of which sent the most aggressive midges choking and recoiling in haste.

Poaching

I no longer think in terms of numbers caught, but of quality, and the excitement of luring and securing a good fish from a most difficult location. In fact, when I now look at one of those native brown trout I feel like returning it to the water, such a beautiful creature out of its natural element. In short, it is no longer the fish, but the art of fishing that appeals to me. But when I look back on my youthful experiences I feel something adventurous has gone out of my fishing. As a friend remarked, 'There's no fun fishing when you have a permit!'

There is a difference between fishing fair for brown trout without permission, and poaching. The first is a pure technicality, the second is how not to catch fish. I have always been curious about the subject, involved as I once was in the occasional cast on the forbidden lochs.

Poaching is the taking of game fish by methods that are illegal or worse. I should explain that although I am interested in the subject, on only one occasion have I illegally experimented. Having heard how deadly was the use of salmon roe as bait, I obtained some, made a paste, and tried it out on a reservoir. Within fifteen minutes I had caught seven or eight trout of all sizes which I returned to the water. This convinced me of the roe's properties.

The poacher of long ago generally worked on his own. The fish he caught were either a useful addition to his family's scanty menu or sold sub judice for the maintenance of his family; for some it was simply for the fun of the escapade. There was even a certain admiration for the genuine poacher who was risking imprisonment for his personal efforts, observing the maxim of the old Highland saying, 'A deer from the hill, a stick from the wood, and a salmon from the pool are the rights of every Highland gentleman.' If he was known to keep his operations within reason and was judicious in the disposal of his product, a sympathetic keeper or policeman might turn a blind eye.

I am also thinking of the poacher who adopts the risky plan of gaffing a salmon or catching it in a long-handled net as it falls back from an unsuccessful leap up a waterfall; and the man who appears to be fishing fairly with the spinner, but the minnow he is using is actually bristling with hooks, and if he feels the slightest touch, he strikes. Then there is the art of using the splash net at the mouth of burns and rivers, or putting down, as Para Handy would say, 'a bit of a net no' the size of a pocket-naipkin', and hanging the catch, wrapped up in pages of *The Oban Times*, behind the cellar doors of the old and needy in the village before they get up in the morning. Long ago when there were no river controls, and salmon was regarded as a monotonous item of food, people used to fish the teeming shoals of salmon using 'leisters' or salmon spears with the light of flaming torches to attract the fish within range. I was given the iron head of one of those murderous weapons which was found in the bed of a Mull river, still well preserved after its long immersion. Such ironwork would be fashioned by the local blacksmiths whom you would find in most of the old communities.

A salmon spear, or 'Leister'. These were made by local blacksmiths

I was very impressed by a skilful device described by a friend in Mull. It is useful if one is just seeking the odd fish. You first locate your salmon in its holding position in about 3ft of water under the bank. If you disturb it, wait, and it will return. Formerly snare wire was used, but now the device is made of fine yellow electric flex, which is so much easier to see and guide. 'Providence's friend to the poacher', my friend called it. You make a noose at one end of it with a sliding knot. You can fix a secure wooden grip to the other end, or simply tie it round your wrist. Tucking up your sleeve, you lower the noose until it is behind the tail of a fish. You ease it along over the tail of the unsuspecting fish until it is encircling its 'wrist', then heave! Either the fish comes flapping on to the bank behind you, or if it is a really large fish and pulls first, you can find yourself splashing in the water!

CHAPTER 6

Local Wildlife

ANGLERS CANNOT AVOID BEING students of wildlife. By river, loch and stream there is so much to see. The very fact that an angler stands fairly still makes some birds and animals so much bolder.

A classic example of this was one day in Loch Carnan nan Amais when I was alone in the boat as usual. I was sitting idly at the oars in a flat calm off what I call Otter Island, a tiny island with a thick covering of overgrown heather. I was no more than ten yards distant when father otter slipped into the water from some holt in the bank, followed by mother otter and three youngsters, paying me not the slightest attention, and they began to swim across the loch. As an experiment, wondering how fast they could swim, I tugged hard at the oars and followed them. Just as I was catching up, the whole family dived as one, reversing right under the boat, came up in its wake, and unhurriedly began to swim back to the island, doubtless expressing their disapproval in otter language. How any so-called sportsmen could ever hunt these loveable creatures with a pack of hounds, and create chaos in a river, beats me.

Another time, when wading and casting along the shallows below the green bank on the opposite side of the same loch, I came across a three-quarters grown hedgehog apparently marooned on a strip of gravel below the bank. It toddled into a deep hole, so I left it and fished on. However, as I was fishing my way back, I noticed two small dark objects moving among the scattered rushes about 10ft off-shore, and looking closer I saw my poor little hedgehog, on its back with just the tip of its nose showing, obviously exhausted. I saved it with my landing net and laid it gently on the grass. When it began to revive I made room in my fishing bag and took it home. It must have fallen off the bank, couldn't get up again, decided to swim along the little beach, and become disoriented. I released it in our garden, hoping it would end the snail and slug menace, but it disappeared soon after. I didn't worry about the fleas which infest many hedgehogs; they don't like humans. Just fancy a hedgehog trying to scratch its back!

I came across the occasional adder, timid little reptiles that melt out of sight when they sense the vibrations of an approaching footfall. In Mull, in spite of its high population of adders, you will rarely see one, except in really hot weather when they love to bask, or when there are young about. They frequent damp sunny areas, such as along the sides of the lochs, where frogs, their principal food, are abundant.

A 2ft adder, the author's least favourite wildlife

The place to look for them is on sun-warmed rocks in one of the little quarries, or on a ruined mossy wall, as I have seen beside Loch Meadhoin. There, after a first disappearing act, I waited with my camera (I often carried it when fishing), and in just a minute or two it materialised – that is the only way I can describe it – and stretched out basking in the sun on the warm moss that matched so well the pattern of its scales. I was able to bring the camera within two feet for a close-up before it reluctantly withdrew.

An adult adder is about 2ft in length, although I have seen them up to 34". They were sometimes killed by the scant traffic in those far-off days of dusty roads on which they liked to bask. I have proved by experiment that the full strike of an average adder from an advantageous coiled position is 10" – but I would not trust an angry adder at less than 2ft. In the past we used to kill those 'serpents' before they could 'sting' you, as the old folk used to say, for they loathed them. I could never kill one now if it was minding its own business.

I was in a birch wood walking quietly on the deep moss watching the fingerling trout. A unique sight was a small adder coiled round a projecting twig sipping water with a bird-like motion from a tiny burn. Once it sensed my presence it withdrew into the bank. Another time, an adder and I both had a fright when I was edging along a shelf on a steep slope. I brought my hand down no more than an inch from one of the fattest and probably longest adders I had ever seen, which fortunately had immediately begun to withdraw in haste when it became aware of me.

One day while fishing a small hill loch in Argyll I saw almost above me a sparrowhawk stooping at speed on an unidentifiable bird that was trying desperately to escape. I heard the impact and saw feathers fly when the sparrowhawk caught up, but it missed its prey with its talons and swerved away; the half-stunned bird dropped quite near me and dragged itself into the thick heather. Hurrying over, I found it was a carrier pigeon with its empty message quill fixed to its leg. I lifted it and took it home, leaving it overnight in a warm dark box. Next morning it was quite perky, eating some grain and obviously practically back to normal. I scribbled a note about the bird's adventure and tucked it into the quill and perched it on a wall outside the house. Presently it flapped its wings, found it could get airborne, and the last I saw of it was a speck merging into the distance.

On a very calm morning on one of the lochs it was amusing to watch a seagull on a little beach trying to teach three or four youngsters to swim. Becoming thoroughly impatient with their lack of co-operation the gull gingered them up with a good pecking!

Once during one of our infrequent hard frosts, when Loch Pellac was frozen all over, I saw a flight of swans came down on the mirror-like surface thinking it was open water. They lay sprawled out for an hour or two, but as I came walking back later they were tottering and sliding about. In the end they all flapped heavily into the air and took off to find a more congenial landing place.

Cormorants sometimes come inland, and my spirits would drop when I came to a loch and saw a cormorant there, or a big diving duck. After doubtless a feed of trout and scaring the others, there was little scope for the angler to follow.

In the sheltered area through which my river ran, I have counted six cuckoos, each with its attendant meadow pipit, between our house and the Falls Pool. Corncrakes used to croak in the rough grass of the damp areas of our ground. The dancing dipper hopped along the stones beside the river. The golden eagle, formerly scarce, is now often seen, its superb soaring distinguishing it from the buzzard. In recent years I have even seen the white-tailed sea eagle over our island, so miles from its habitat on the island of Rum, where pairs are gradually being introduced from Scandinavia.

No reference to wildlife and in particular the persecution of anglers would be complete without mentioning the midges. Active round any boggy shore, especially in the evening when the wind falls away, they are not nearly so bad out on the water (which is another reason why I prefer to fish from a boat!). Another excellent place to find midges, perhaps best of all, is in the same, calm conditions along the upper layers of rotting seaweed lining the shores. However, I have found the perfect answer, being a person to whom appearances mean nothing. I hang a net of the finest green nylon mesh from the brim of my hat, well tucked in everywhere. It interferes surprisingly little with vision, as long as you can part the veils of frustrated midges on the outside! Fortunately, when even a light breeze gets up, midges vanish.

There are no foxes in Mull. But rabbits used to be so numerous, and such a common item of food, that I shall quote the words of a disgruntled farmer who was once asked by the visiting minister to say a thanksgiving after a meal where rabbit had appeared prominently on the menu:

Rabbits young and rabbits old,
Rabbits hot and rabbits cold,
Rabbits tender and rabbits tough,
I thank the Lord I've had enough.

CHAPTER 7

Sporting Pastimes

DURING MY BOYHOOD Mull used to benefit considerably from the letting of sporting rights, especially stalking, which is still important today. One notable figure who took the shootings on Torosay estate was Count von Leichtenstein who drove an old, rather rare, three-litre open Bentley motor car and was a menace on our narrow roads. A popular figure, he once acted as chairman at a concert in the Aros Hall, and I still remember part of his speech when he admired the island of Mull and compared it with his own rugged country.

The golden days of the sporting estates are over, with the mounting costs of staffing, the deterioration or disappearance of the heather that used to support the grouse population, and hill areas reduced by afforestation. Certainly you do get deer in many isolated corners of Mull. I have watched a small herd coming down at dusk to raid the young growing crops in Glenbellart at Dervaig. An old experienced hind was always the leader on such a foray, her ears, as I watched, twitching against the glow of the sunset, and only when she gave the all clear would the rest move down.

There were even coveys of grouse on the moor around our house near Tobermory. Now they are gone. Pheasants are still reared (for instance, within the policies of Torosay Castle), but we used to see them in the wild from our windows.

The Game of Golf

Between 1909 and 1914 there was a sudden enthusiasm for the game of golf in Mull. Three holes were even laid out on the highly preserved machair at Calgary, and several at

The author on Old Tobermory Golf Course c. 1920

Glengorm, while Iona had something more substantial. They all faded out except for the course on Iona. Post-war a nine-hole course was laid out around the hill above old Aros Castle at Salen, and nine holes were created at Torosay on some very boggy land. Again, both more or less disappeared, but in the 1960s Torosay revived and is now an active little club.

The Tobermory Golf Club was founded in 1896. Play started first of all on Erray estate land lying just beyond the Western Isles Hotel above Tobermory Bay. Two years later the course was moved to grazing land lying between Sgriobruadh Farm and Achafraoch House a mile up the Dervaig road. However, the affairs of the Club lapsed in 1900; but in 1907 it started up again with renewed enthusiasm on the same site, where it remained until 1935, with one re-arrangement of holes. It then moved to a new course of eighteen holes laid out by David Adam and run by the Western Isles Hotel, after which the new club was named; but in 1947, after World War II, it was reduced to nine holes through financial and practical difficulties of upkeep.

There were thus two clubs in the Burgh, the Western Isles Golf Club and the original Tobermory Golf Club, and they combined under the traditional name in 1987. Land was purchased in 1988, a new club house built in 1992, and it is now one of the most picturesque of any of the golf courses in the Western Isles, perhaps in Scotland. Its official length is 2,460 yards (2,249 m), par 64. It is on the short side by accepted standards, but that is fully compensated for by the excellent natural turf, and the good amenities and maintenance. So, thanks to the hard work, persistence and enthusiasm of a small body of people, the primitive course we knew in the 1920s is now a prestigious golf club.

However, it is of that challenging course up the Dervaig road that I have nostalgic memories, for it lay just a mashie shot from our land. Short and cramped, but a formidable challenge, if off line. Today I still enjoy that straightness of execution envied by my less fortunate partners and I attribute this to the instinctive control imposed on me by the dread risk of losing a ball in my formative years.

We had rocks, bracken, heather, ruins, walls, a bog, grazing cattle and fenced greens ('Re-play is permitted if a stroke is interfered with by wire or posts'), yet we held inter-club games there with Salen, Craignure, and even the (now closed) Ganavan Club from Oban. The sixth hole was of special note for me. Before I had an interest in golf, we boys used to tuck up our sleeves and investigate the water-filled hoof marks left by cattle in the soft peat – the golf balls seemed to prefer these to the players' objective on the green. But if an off-line ball missed those holes and the other hazards, it could bounce off the main road, out of bounds, and finish up in a corner of our field. Here, by coincidence, my father always grew oats or hay, or some other impenetrable crop, for, as he explained when apologising to the golfers, this was the most fertile land of his five acres. He also assured suspicious golf club members that the barbed wire stretched along the top of the wall was to keep out marauding deer that damaged the crops. This might well have been true, for we once saw a stag outlined against the sky some distance away, and deer did jump over the wall at the other side of the house and nibble the tops of young trees.

As a result, we had two crops from that field. My preference was for golf balls, for I had taken up the game in 1919. I admit that neither my father nor I ever had to buy a golf ball until, much to my disgust, I was forced to do so when I moved away. I became a golf ball connoisseur. This was the time of experiments between the 'gutty' and the modern, and it had not been very long since a player was permitted to drop another ball without penalty on the spot where the largest portion of his ball in play had come to rest. There were floaters like the Patent Colonel, or bullet-like balls such as the North British. There were many different names, and I still have a (found) ball stamped 'Baby Dimple'. Balls were dimpled, brambled, latticed, starred, even hacked and sliced (although these latter features were not designed by the makers). The best could cost as much as 1/6 (7½p) or even 2/- (10p).

Our golf clubs were an unmatched assortment, and the wooden clubs had hickory shafts and persimmon heads. The others had the same kind of shaft, but iron heads that rusted and had to be kept polished with emery cloth, apart from the striking faces which we left rough, even punched, for this was alleged to give the ball better backspin, a practice officially banned years later when it became so prevalent that the cover was nearly dragged off the ball.

Iron clubs cost from 7/6 (37½p) upwards, woods slightly more. There were none of your impersonal numbers! From driver downwards we had brassie, spoon, baffy, then driving iron, mid iron, cleek, mashie, niblick and putter. With no limits to the number of clubs, you could add Number 2 and 3 mashies, mashie-iron, mashie-niblick and a sand iron like a navvy's spade.

When I was treasurer of the Tobermory Golf Club in the 1920s, the cost of a day's golf was 1/- (5p), the annual membership fee 15/- (75p), and the members numbered about 50. I forget the number of lady members and their fees. In the last years of this century the corresponding fees are £10 and £60!

Since golf was almost as much of an obsession of mine as angling, it was inevitable that I would win something sometime. I particularly remember winning the Navy Cup in the years 1923 and 1924 because of the happy and sad history of that cup. A year or two before World War 1 Tobermory had a visit from the 5th Cruiser Squadron under Admiral Sir Christopher Cradock. In return for the usual courtesy use of our golf course, the officers presented us with a handsome silver cup for an annual knock-out competition. We named it the Navy Cup.

When World War I broke out, the 5th Cruiser Squadron was sent at once to the Pacific, to dispose of German units that were posing a major threat to allied shipping in the East. There was a powerful squadron of modern heavy German cruisers. They met up with the Admiral's old, out-dated cruisers on the 1st November, 1914, off the coast of Coronel, Chile. Out-ranged and out-sailed, our ships suffered a major defeat, with the loss of HMS *Monmouth* and *Good Hope* and the death of Admiral Cradock.

However, retribution followed. On 8th December, 1914, Von Spee's squadron attacked the Falkland Islands to destroy the important wireless station situated there, unaware of the presence of a powerful British unit that included the battlecruiser *HMS Invincible*. Von Spee tried to retire, but too late. After a courageous fight every German ship except the *Dresden* (destroyed soon after) was out-ranged and sunk by the massive 12" guns of the battlecruiser. Our fighting ships had only 35 casualties!

Yachts and Yachting

Yachting has always been a popular sport in the ideal situation of Tobermory Bay. The Regatta used to be the favourite annual event, with rowing, and swimming and other associated sports. It has been replaced by the equally popular annual Tobermory Games.

Long ago many luxury steam yachts used to anchor in the Bay, symbols of undreamed-of luxuries and a way of life quite alien to us. We came to know the names of those impressive visitors.

Biggest and finest of them all, with her yellow funnel and

dazzling white, was the *Iolaire* (Eagle), belonging, I think, to the Runcimans of Eigg. She used to anchor in the deep water off Drumfin House on the south side of the Bay. Requisitioned for service during World War I, her last voyage was to Stornoway with a large contingent of soldiers and sailors happily returning home, the war at an end for them. This was in the very last hours of 1918. There then occurred the saddest of tragedies that shocked the Long Island (Lewis and Harris) and the whole nation. As the ship was about to enter Stornoway harbour, within sight of the lights of home, she struck heavily on the notorious reef, 'The Beasts of Holm', and sank in a few minutes with the loss of 205 service men. At the public enquiry that followed the captain and crew were found guilty of gross negligence.

CHAPTER 8

Getting About

The Arrival of the Motor Car

THE ROADS ON MULL in the early days of the 20th century were somewhat different from those in the latter years of the century. The road system is the same, but there the similarity ends, for the coming of the motor car transformed both the quality and the design.

Most of the roads followed the easiest land contours to suit the earlier horse-drawn vehicles, and there were innumerable blind corners, gradients, narrows, and deep drainage ditches. Many roads evolved from the still earlier drove roads

The road between Tobermory and Dervaig with Loch Frisa in the distance.
A challenging climb by car or bike.

(cattle roads), traces of which can still be seen on the Ordnance Survey maps. An interesting path crosses the shoulder of Ben More at the head of Glen Chlachaig linking Loch Scridain with Loch na Keal. This was an important link, by-passing Gribun, and from the small portions of its construction still remaining, it is thought that light carts may even have crossed over, drawn by two horses. Some years ago it was crossed by motor cycle as an adventure. It is now an official Right of Way.

Many of the tracks on the maps seem to go nowhere, but they connected the old centres of population that were swept away by the Clearances, leaving nothing but an occasional ruin. For instance, there are the tracks across the hills and moors centring on the former school house of Reudle, that gaunt shell standing above the Torloisk to Treshnish road, one of the most remote in Mull. This school was attended by pupils from miles around, to whom the distance from home to school meant nothing. You can still see the graffiti of old sailing ships on what remains of the plastered walls of the schoolroom.

Maintenance of these roads, many of whose surfaces were water-bound, was a steady job for roadmen who often had to walk many miles to and from the section for which they were responsible. As fast as potholes appeared, they had to be filled in with coarse road metal blinded with 'rotten rock' and rolled in, if possible, by horse-drawn road roller. I often watched the men at work in the roadside quarries, extracting slabs of rock with crowbars and breaking them down with graduated weights of hammer until the final 'knapping' down into road metal. As boys we were somewhat frightened of these men with their dark protective mesh glasses. Their work was piled into heaps to be assessed by the roads foreman or surveyor, for payment was by piece work. Hammer handles were replaced with lengths of the abundant

A road gang on the Dervaig road in the 1920s

hazel. Dozens of their little quarries are still to be seen by the roadsides, now all overgrown. The old roadmen were amateur geologists, knowledgeable about the quality of the basalt rocks, the most easily worked cleavage planes and the jointing for breaking down. They tapped away for tireless hours with wrists that must have been like steel.

Before my father left the island to join the Hong Kong Police Force, about the year 1880 he carted every one of the twelve milestones between Tobermory and Calgary. Square blocks of red Ross of Mull granite, they are all still in position.

In dry weather the early motor cars used to pass over the roads in a cloud of dust, and in rainy conditions in showers of muddy spray. With the introduction of a binding bituminised surface, all this changed, and nowadays road work is concentrated in a few large quarries worked by modern methods, with organised gangs of roadmen who travel by lorry which carries equipment, road metal, and fine top dressing brought in by ship from the Bonawe quarries on Loch Etive, and big containers of bitumen for the finer hard smooth surface.

The early, pre-World War 1 cars, owned by the gentry, were often great perambulating parlours, gleaming with polished brass, where the chauffeur sat unprotected from the weather behind a vertical windscreen, at the end of a speaking tube. There were models such as the Minerva, Delaunay-Belville, Panhard-Levasseur and others – built long before the years of mass production. Audible warning of approach was delivered by a sneering horn operated by a bulb attached to a long tube like an anaconda outside the bonnet. Regular use had to be made of those horns, especially at blind corners, with likely obstacles such as cattle or another vehicle. Brakes were not quite as efficient then, nor were tyres, which suffered from the rough metalled surface.

Electric lamps were slow to appear on cars; first there was the feeble paraffin lamp, then the more efficient acetylene, from a container generating the gas from calcium carbide and a drip of water. Such illumination was nearly adequate for the slow speeds of the motor cars. The popular cars of the 1920s, for example the Morris and the Austin, had a maximum speed of around 50 mph with improvements being made all the time. As a relic of the past, for many years a post stood at the Burgh boundary above the town stating that the maximum speed permissible within the Burgh was 10 mph.

The price of a car then was between £200 and £300. In 1934 I acquired a second-hand Swift two-seater of 1928 vintage. It was of slightly better class, costing £350 new. We could identify from a distance the individual makes of our old models, especially the rakish unmistakability of the old sports cars! I ran mine for fun for 40 years, until it became a cynosure for the public eye. I only gave it up in the interests of the comfort and performance of a modern car. I called that car Rosinante, after the broken-down hack ridden by the great Don Quixote, of whose vagaries I was frequently accused.

A superior characteristic of these old vehicles was their sturdy construction of heavy gauge steel built on to a solid frame and made to last. The engines expired before the bodies, although the engines were so accessible that owner-maintenance was easy for most people. A welcome improvement came with the elimination of the 'beaded' tyre whose removal was a real headache.

I had acquired a motor cycle when I moved to Glasgow and before Rosinante appeared; it sticks in my memory, because in 1928 the price of petrol fell to a figure of 11 pence – about 5p in decimal currency. A year later it shot up by tuppence to 1/1 amid screams of protest when the then Chancellor of the Exchequer, Winston Churchill, imposed the tax to start off the Road Fund. With my motor-bike I could explore half of Scotland for 10p!

No reference to motoring in the 1920s and 1930s would be complete without mentioning the apparently simple act of driving a car on and off the Sound of Mull mailboat. Before side-loading ships and suitable piers were designed, the operation involved the first officer in person and the whole crew, and always drew the same type of crowd you see at rallies and racing tracks – waiting for a catastrophe.

First the crew eyed the width of your car's wheels and set two wide planks the correct distance apart between pier and deck. The first officer, well back out of reach on the deck, stood with raised finger. Then gingerly you let in the clutch, and pretending you had an egg under the foot pedals, began to edge either up or down the planks – the tide saw to it they were never horizontal. Fixing your eye on the officer's guiding finger, you steered white-faced across the 20ft deep gap with the water surging hungrily below. If the planks were at

Driving 'the planks'. The author unloading his car, Rosinante, in 1936.

too acute an angle up or down, the crew would seize the ends and raise or lower them as you braked gently on to the deck. Safely aboard, the crew then 'bounced' the car on its springs out of the way. Sometimes the tide might be too high or too low at Tobermory for this loading operation, but in such circumstances you could drive the 12 miles to Salen pier, and by the time the ship arrived there, the tide had relented and you could board.

Less nerve-shattering was the later method whereby you drove the car on to a thick padded mat with ropes at each corner which was carefully hoisted up and slung on board by the ship's derrick. Simplicity in boarding came with a side-loading ramp on the ship enabling the car to be driven on board and turned on a turntable to take its place in a queue on the deck, then to be unloaded by the same procedure. In my long experience I never heard of a single incident in embarking or disembarking. Now you might say that the road continues onto the ship with modern roll-on roll-off facilities.

I do believe that those picturesque herds of Highland cattle which wander along the main roads respond only to the Gaelic, for they ignore the horn blast with studied indifference, as well as the invective hurled at them by drivers hurrying to catch the ferry. All you need to do is to lower a window and bellow 'MACH-E' (get out), to send them thundering off.

'Loading' a car onto the ferry – before the modern RO-RO car ferry

Ships and Shipping

As an island race the people of Mull have always depended on the sea roads for communications.

During the first quarter of the 20th century a great variety of boats and ships served the island. The auxiliary engine was being installed in lobster boats and suchlike, but skiffs and sailing smacks were still much to the fore inter-island. Chief among the larger ships were those of the David MacBrayne fleet – now Caledonian MacBrayne, or simply Cal-Mac. The company today is owned by the Secretary of State for Scotland, for the financial difficulties that developed as the century went on were too much for a private company to face, and the service to the Isles is indispensable.

The real turning point in sea travel to the islands came in 1880 when the Caledonian Railway reached Oban, and Mull shared some of its reflected radiance. From 1881 a daily mailboat ran between Tobermory and Oban. This service ran until 1964 when the new car ferry terminus was established at Craignure, which took over from Tobermory as the main point of disembarkation.

The Mailboat

No reference to MacBrayne and the Tobermory-to-Oban daily run would be complete without tales of the old *MV Lochinvar*, that uncouth-looking, fast, tough motor vessel of about 300 tons, which was based at Tobermory, and with which Mull people had a love-hate relationship. She was one of the earliest of the fleet to depart from steam. She took over the run in 1909 from the old *Carabineer*. Originally fitted with an exhaust like a thin factory chimney, she acquired three exhausts in a triangle sticking up from the deck; if you were knowledgeable, the warmest spot on deck was leaning against one of these on the lee side. Tough in spite of her flimsy appearance, she once sank a fishing boat that had unwisely anchored in a fog off Craignure, her sharp bow none the worse; and she did it again in Oban near the entrance to the Bay – fortunately with no loss of life in either case.

There were two classes of accommodation for passengers – cabin and steerage – and if Jimmy Black, the Purser, was on

The first appearance at Tobermory Pier in 1909 of the new mailboat, *MV Lochinvar*

his toes, never would the twain meet. In the 1920s the return fare steerage, Tobermory/Oban, was 7/6 (37½p) and cabin 15/- (75p). The affluent sat in the cushioned comfort of the stateroom forward, with seven pictures round the walls of the adventures of the Young Lochinvar of poetic memory. The transport charges for livestock were 1/- for a sheep and sixpence for a dog.

I remember seeing Jimmy Black open the door of a huge Rolls Royce belonging to some wealthy laird or sporting tenant, and demand sixpence for the tiny lapdog held by the aristocratic lady who chose to remain in the comfort of the car for the voyage. This incident occurred just after the ship returned from a major refit and looked rather more spruce, with a single stumpy exhaust funnel and a deck crane forward with a notice which read 'LOAD NOT TO EXCEED FIVE TONS'.

In wild weather the run to Oban could be something of an ordeal for steerage passengers, who were obliged to shelter in the open on hard benches in the 'tween deck under the bridge structure, with the damp sea-winds blowing freely round them. Nor was that all they had to suffer. The accommodation was within range of the open door to the engine room, from which fumes of hot oil and diesel fuel poured without interruption, and was close to the crew's galley where kippers would be frying with a lovely aroma, ready for the crew's breakfast. This was no joke when the ship reached the tide-rip off Lismore lighthouse, corkscrewing across the water with the inevitable gale on her beam.

Add to all that a seasonal cargo of wet, smelly sheep bound for the Oban market. Imagine the chaos, with up to 1,000 sheep (I've counted them without falling asleep) packed into the steerage space sometimes to a point when the purser grudgingly allowed us to move to the cabin accommodation – without paying the extra. Up on the bridge at Salen and Lochaline, where the sheep were loaded, the red-faced skipper would lean over the side, screaming imprecations about the time being lost, which might cause the ship to miss the midday mail train from Oban to Glasgow.

The author's banking colleague landing his Ariel, with side-car, at Oban from
MV Lochinvar in 1928.

I remember the consternation that swept Tobermory one wild day in the depths of winter, when the *Lochinvar* literally disappeared after leaving Oban. The crew were nearly all Tobermory men with wives and families there. What had happened was that a howling gale was blowing up the Firth of Lorne, so severe that the captain, proud as he was of his time-keeping, dared not leave the pier at Oban. However, during a lull he had set off, hoping to reach the shelter of Mull, but half-way across the storm had resumed even more fiercely.

Unable to turn the ship back to Oban or fight her way onwards, even with her engines going flat out, the skipper eased her round until the elements were astern, and in the darkness she was blown away up through the islands and narrows of Loch Linnhe. Taken through by a magnificent display of seamanship, she dropped anchor in the first reasonable shelter they came to and waited for daylight. The captain found his ship was in a safe situation somewhere near Fort William, as far from Oban as Tobermory, but in the wrong direction! The news of her escape from the storm was telegraphed in the morning and brought a huge wave of relief to the whole Mull community.

There were, of course, glorious summer days when the Sound of Mull was as smooth as glass, reflecting the incredibly blue mountains of Mull and beyond.

The *Lochinvar* was a friendly ship. Sometimes when there was a local couple on board returning from their honeymoon, she would be bedecked with bunting, every flag flying, from the Blue Peter to 'I have yellow fever on board'. There is a story of an excited wee boy waiting beside his mother on the pier: 'Look, look, there comes the *Lochinvar* full of flags.' Another more prosaic tale is of the exchange of news between two Tobermory worthies: 'Did you see anybody coming on the boat today?' 'Oh, yes, there wass a chentleman, two cows, and a commercial traveller.'

Perhaps somewhat unwisely the ship used to sail on New Year's Day, when the crew could hardly be expected to have one eye open after Hogmanay. When the crane man went into action to raise a heifer from the small ferryboat at Craignure on to the deck, he became a little confused. He managed to raise the poor beast above deck level, but could not remember how to halt the rotation of the crane. So, there was the terrified bellowing heifer rotating over the boat, the pier and the Sound of Mull, until the operator shouted up to the bridge, 'Hey, Captain, will you stop the boat turning round so that I can lower the beast to the deck?'

The *Lochinvar* had a sad end. Sold to a company in the south, and on her way to take up excursion cruising on the east coast, she was wrecked in a gale off the Yorkshire coast and was a total loss. However, her binnacle was saved and is displayed in Duart Castle.

Although the atmosphere has vanished from the Oban to Mull ferry run, eliminated by modern sophistication, 1,000 passengers, 100 cars, lounges, a restaurant and promenade decks, and the happy chatty days on the pier are no more, there is still one place in which you might see a familiar face from the old days – the bar!

Indispensable as the service is throughout the Hebrides, Caledonian MacBrayne comes in for plenty of criticism. Their near monopoly is described in the following terms:-

> The earth belongs unto the Lord
> And all that it contains,
> Except for all the Western Isles
> And they are the MacBrayne's.

Early Vessels of the MacBrayne Fleet

In the early days MacBrayne had a fleet of about 35 ships, from the big *PS Columba*, the 'Pride of the Clyde', to the tiny *Handa*. The 1,000 tons vessels, the *Chieftain* and *Claymore*, sailed from the Broomielaw in Glasgow to Stornoway, calling at ports along the route. In 1900, for a return fare of £9 cabin, ie, first class, you could travel to Stornoway and back, with an optional break at Oban, where you could travel from Oban to Fort William, and thence through the Caledonian Canal and back with the *PS Gondolier*, to be picked up at Oban again as the ship returned from Stornoway. Smaller vessels like the *Dirk* and the *Shiela* dodged round the lesser ports of call.

At the time of the seasonal livestock sales at Oban, small ships of the MacBrayne fleet such as the *Princess-Louise* used

Unloading coal. The flat-bottomed puffer beached at high tide to allow the carts to come alongside.

A puffer tied up alongside Tobermory Pier in the 1940s

to call at tiny piers in places like Calgary, where they picked up the cattle and sheep that otherwise would have had to be driven across Mull all the way to the Sound of Mull ports. Now, of course, livestock are carried in large floats, taken across by drive-on drive-off ferry and delivered direct to the markets.

MacBrayne had only one competitor, McCallum Orme, (later taken over), whose more adventurous sailings by the *Hebrides* and *Hebridean* sometimes reached as far as St Kilda. For years I was puzzled by the derivation of that name, for there is no Saint Kilda. The problem was solved by a lady familiar with the history of the Vikings, who pointed out that the name came from two words in the Old Norse, *Sunt* (fresh or healthy) and *Kilde* (a source of water), for Hirta (the other name for St Kilda) was an island where the roving Vikings could pick up fresh water.

There were also fast paddle steamers, most of whose

names ended in 'eer' or 'eir' such as the *Grenadier*, a popular cruise ship on the daily run from Oban to Staffa and Iona. She was partly destroyed by fire, with the loss of her captain, beside Oban pier on 6 September 1927. I remember once joining the *Grenadier* at Tobermory, sailing on her to Iona, crossing the small ferry to the mainland of Mull, and cycling the 50 miles home to Tobermory.

The puffers (or '*Vital Sparks*'!) were the workhorses for bulk cargoes such as coal, sand, etc. They were able to creep into all kinds of places, beach themselves at high tide and unload into carts driven alongside. The 'puffing' was of course the exhaust steam puffing from the donkey engine as it manipulated the hoists.

CHAPTER 9

Mull at War

I WAS ELEVEN YEARS OF AGE when World War I broke out. A great black cloud seemed to come down over the community, above all when the appalling lists of casualties started to appear. We began to lose something of our faith in the invincibility of our forces. Or it may have been that civilians felt themselves so helpless. The '39 – '45 war was different, for in spite of the massive threats from air and sea, civilians were involved in the fight as Wardens and Home Guards, and in the Observers' Corps, Fire Service, the Women's Land Army, Nursing, and many more occupations.

In my case, the products of my romantic reading received a rude shock, the worst being after the battle of Jutland, when it was claimed that the German gunnery was superior to ours. It was many years before I was reassured, for apparently the Germans had been using armour-piercing shells, whereas for some reason we used mainly impact-exploding shells. The prices of my weekly and monthly boys' magazines began to escalate, going up by as much as 50%. Tuppence instead of one penny weekly was quite a drain on my slender resources, and the monthly threepenny magazine went up to fourpence and more!

My brother Robin, who was a medical student at Edinburgh University and had been in the Territorials, was called up at once. Every day we feared the arrival of the dreaded letter or telegram, knowing that he was in the thick of the fighting near Neuve Chapelle and Festubert. At one point his section of the 4th Camerons (now disbanded) had been cut off, having to escape along a flooded ditch. (Later he showed us his kilt and haversack, shot through with machine gun bullets.) He had a miraculous escape. Soon after this he was recalled to his studies at Edinburgh, because of the increasing demand for doctors.

Twice after his home leave my father and I travelled with him to see him off, once to Edinburgh and once to Glasgow. These were my first visits to the two cities. We travelled on the Caledonian Railway by way of Callander and Stirling. My first impressions of Glasgow in the winter time were of bright lights, rain, a bewildering combination of tram cars in assorted colours with vivid sparks from the overhead lines, greasy pavements, smoke, hurrying crowds and the shouts from newsboys at the street corners.

Edinburgh was more sedate, spacious, and dignified. It was eerie at night on some of the outlying deserted streets to hear the rumble under the ground of the cable running between the tramlines that hauled the tram cars along. Waverley Station was the main arrival point for the leave trains from the south. As we were standing there, one of the leave trains drew in at Platform Number 1, hauled by a great Pacific engine. I can still see the poor exhausted soldiers stumbling out of the coaches, bowed down with rifles and kit, with the mud of Flanders still on their puttees and greatcoats. What a war that was. Conducted by generals bogged down in outdated traditions, it was indeed fortunate that the German High Command was not much better. Even more did we respect that Mull laird, a General in the Highland Division, who when ordered to send his men into some impossible attack, refused to do so, saying bluntly he was not prepared to have his men murdered for nothing. And he got away with it!

Before World War 1 there was a drill hall in Tobermory on the road where the Police Office is now situated. Here the local Volunteers used to drill and practice with .22 rifles and long and short types of ammunition. Enthusiasm in Tobermory for the '39-'45 war effort was so strong that even the picturesque old cannon that had stood along the Lighthouse road, probably since the time of the Napoleonic wars, was sacrificed for its weight in valuable iron. There are still two smaller cannons on Mull, one on Bellachroy Hill at Dervaig, now to be mounted and displayed in front of the new village hall, the other on Penmore hill. The Armouries of the Tower of London, the authority on the subject, considered they were coastal defence cannons installed during the Napoleonic Wars. On a few special occasions the Bellachroy cannon was charged with powder by some of the lads of the village and discharged with a satisfactory bang.

Tobermory and its environs had the proud distinction that during World War II it became the most important and successful base in Britain for training in anti-submarine tactics. You can read all about it in Richard Baker's book, *The Terror of Tobermory*, the Terror being Vice-Admiral Stephenson (familiarly known as 'Puggy' or 'Monkey Brand') who was knighted for his work. Under his exacting and unorthodox methods, no less than 1,000 ships, from destroyer size downwards, and 250,000 men passed through his hands. Between them they accounted for 130 German U-boats and 40 aircraft.

During the First World War Tobermory was the base for five old cruisers whose duties were to patrol the area. One morning as I went to school I heard a distant B O O M echoing across the moorlands that set every cock grouse cackling in alarm. That night only four ships returned. One had hit a mine and sunk.

We had scares about U-boats around Mull. We were once virtually cut off for a week after sailings were suspended to the mainland, and were running short of essentials before normality was resumed. It was about this time that the Barra mailboat was chased and shelled ineffectually by a U-boat.

Just fancy the ignorance of a German captain who thought he could outwit a MacBrayne skipper in his own waters!

In the book *A Ring of Bright Water* by the late Gavin Maxwell, you will read the story about a Barra boat skipper, a forthright Hebridean with a high-pitched voice which gave him his nickname of The Squeaker. During the war a fussy wee admiral in mufti was on board the boat on his way to the Outer Islands. Being somewhat apprehensive about the course of the boat in relation to certain minefields he thought he remembered, he went up to the bridge, to be greeted with 'Get off my plotty bridge' from The Squeaker, who was shocked by this invasion of his preserve. However, when the admiral introduced himself, the Squeaker became genial and said, 'Come on down, atmiral, and we'll haf a glass'.

They went down to the captain's quarters, where the worried admiral expressed his fears. 'Have you a chart of the area?' he enquired. The Squeaker produced a pile of charts, starting with the South China Sea and the English Channel, and finally found a much-tattered chart of the Minches. The admiral traced their course, then exclaimed in an agitated voice, 'Look, these dots represent the new minefield right across our course.' The Squeaker eyed the chart with contempt, took another sip at his glass, and replied, 'Atmiral, if these iss mines we're b*****ed; but if they are what I think – chust fly-shit, we're aal right.'

Another good story of a different kind emerged in Tobermory during the war when butchers were permitted in an emergency to do their own slaughtering of livestock, instead of ordering meat to be sent from Oban. One day a local butcher went into the Post Office to send a telegram to Oban, and gave the message to the formidable and efficient lady then in charge. When he left and another local man came in, she remarked – with that secrecy observed by some small country offices, 'Isn't that a stupid telegram to be sending to Oban: "Don't send meat am killing myself."' The new-comer thought this over for a long time and delivered his verdict, 'Inteet, yess, it iss stupid. I'm sure he couldn't be killing himself without a licence.'

Tobermory Bay was a sheltered haven where ships damaged by mines or torpedoes could get patched up for the haul down to the teeming shipyards of the Clyde. Some beached themselves temporarily and we could see enormous holes in their sides.

The occasional drifting mine detonated round our coast, such as the one tackled by Alick Ban. The only incident of note was the one that exploded at the entrance to Fingal's Cave in Staffa and brought down a mass of columns.

In both wars Loch na Keal in the west of Mull was a secure assembly place for convoys, and during World War 1 it was a strategic anchorage for the Grand Fleet. The war really came home to us on the 27th January 1918 when the liner *Aurania*, requisitioned for war duties, sank against the southern extension of the cliffs of Caliach. Fortunately, this happened on her return journey to the USA, after landing a large contingent of troops from overseas. She had been torpedoed off the Irish coast south of the Mull of Kintyre, beached apparently in a sinking condition, but refloated. She was hardly taken in tow when the tow rope parted, and for some strange reason she was allowed to drift north to her end against the Caliach cliffs.

During the Second World War we were alarmed to realise how close we were to the activities of German long-range aircraft. The *SS Breda* was lying with other ships gathering to make up a convoy quite near Oban, just across the Firth of Lorne from Mull. On 23rd December, 1940, the group was attacked by two Heinkel bombers. Bombs were dropped on the *Breda*, the main target at 4,500 tons, and carrying a valuable cargo. Although the bombs missed, the explosions alongside were so violent that the ship was severely damaged, and she had to be beached. Unfortunately, she slipped off into deep water and was lost.

In Kilmore cemetery at Dervaig and at several other cemeteries plots were set aside with headstones inscribed *To the Unknown Sailor* for those whose bodies were washed up on the shores after ocean tragedies.

In Tobermory during the First World War we were reasonably well fed, for we could fall back on local produce that helped to eke out the main commodities. As a growing boy the shortage of sugar was a grievous loss. However, my father kept bees and this was when they came into their own! Before the war there had been little demand for his produce and he could expect to receive no more than sixpence (2½p) for a perfect pound section of heather honey. My mother unearthed a mini-churn, and by skimming the thin layer of cream off the milk, she gathered enough to fill the vessel. Then we took it in turn to thump the tiny plunger up and down until – oh, joy! – we had a delicious pat of real fresh butter. We had ample vegetables, and poultry and eggs to spare. My mother used to send boxes of eggs – secured in fancy clips – to the military hospitals in the south. Local fish were sometimes available, and even my trout were welcome.

Another of our war efforts was collecting sphagnum moss from the neighbouring boglands, spreading it out to dry on the floor of one of the big empty wards in Achafraoch House and picking it clean of all detritus. It was in great demand in hospitals on account of its absorbent and aseptic characteristics for dressing wounds. We were able to repeat this service in the Second World War, gathering the moss from deep beds on the inland moors.

The water supply to Tobermory pier was quite inadequate to meet the needs of the Royal and Merchant Navies. We used to see the naval ships collecting fresh water at the foot of the Sput Dubh, as we called the little waterfall that drops over the low cliff straight into the sea beside the path leading to Drumfin House. After the war a figure of £300,000 was required to restore the pier to a safe condition, and neither MacBrayne (which owned it), the Admiralty, nor the County Council would face up to the problem for many years.

Perhaps my most lasting memory from the First World War was when we accompanied a friend of the family, Captain Charles Maclean, to our gate on the evening before his departure once again for the front. I still see his face in the moonlight and hear his sad farewell: 'I'll not be coming back.' Nor did he. He lies in Flanders.

CHAPTER 10

Early Days in the Bank

THE BEST WAY TO DESCRIBE what banking was like in the first quarter of the century is to tell you about my own early years.

On the 10th day of April 1922 I sidled diffidently into the Tobermory branch of the bank I was to serve for the next 41 years. At the age of 18½ I was rather old for admission, but I was accepted on my scholastic record. A severe illness had denied me a start in journalism, and I was unable to take up a university course in medicine like my elder brother, for the family had no spare cash left. So, as the Victorians used to say – and my parents were Victorian – 'As the boy showed no business ability whatever, we put him in a bank'. I wasn't greatly taken with the idea at first, for my ambitions ran along the lines of the romantic poem by Charles Kingsley:

Na, Ah widna be a clerk, mither, tae bide always ben,
Scribblin' ower sheets o' parchment wi' a weary, weary
  pen,
Lookin' through the lang stane windows at a narrow strip
  o' sky,
Like a laverock in a withy cage until Ah pine awa' an'
  die.

However, looking back on it, it was all for the best, and I was happy at my work – well, most of the time. Observing the banking dictum to 'Hear, speak and see no evil', I will not name the bank, although its identity may soon emerge.

As a junior apprentice, I was dogsbody. All the day's letters and lists were written in copying ink and had to be brutally squeezed between the dampened pages of a 'letter book' in the jaws of a massive press. Woe betide me if one of the originals became smudged, particularly any letter written to customers in the copperplate hand of Archibald McGilp, the agent. He was a fine man, a local, and a fluent Gaelic speaker. We had no telephone, no typewriter and no mechanical aids whatsoever. Later in life a colleague in Tobermory once said to me, 'The biggest curse that ever came to the office was the telephone. Here's me trying to tide a man I know well over the winter with a wee overdraft, and Head Office comes on the 'phone telling me I am not to do it!'

Our staff consisted of the agent, the accountant and me. For agent, read manager, a more appropriate title introduced some years later. In those days there were non-banker agents, such as lawyers and accountants, who could bring good per-

The former office of the Clydesdale Bank where the author began his banking career in 1922. Next to it is the Italian Warehouse belonging to Baillie John Fletcher, the "Italian" title of which was a puzzle to us as schoolboys.

sonal business to the bank. These appointments over the heads of senior bank staff who were more than capable of being appointed themselves were strongly resented, and the bank gradually eliminated them in favour of a 100% banking staff.

Years of experience were required behind the scenes before you were thought fit for the duties of teller (the Scottish name for cashier), dealing directly with the public across the counter. However, in a small office like ours, I was soon thrown in at the deep end when the agent was upstairs and the accountant out for lunch. There was no lunchtime closing in those days and the word 'security' had not come into business use. I could always have rung for the manager to come downstairs to solve a problem, but I don't think such an emergency ever arose.

What tellers aimed for was accurate speed, to save waiting time for customers. I wonder how a modern teller would face up to my job in another office where I was in sole charge of the counter. On busy days we had the usual crowd of customers, but superimposed on that were occasions when I had up to 300 individual fuel accounts presented for payment, practically every one involving change from a £1 note upwards – with no mechanical aid whatsoever.

It took me a month to master that fast, elusive flick of the fingers that seemed peculiar to Scottish tellers. Later, when I was in Head Office, and the first note-counting machine was installed, it was challenged by an expert teller; but while he could hold his own for the first £1,000, his fingers slowed and tired in competition with the tireless rubber fingers of the machine. We were still using the last of the flimsy £1 and 10/- notes issued during World War I to replace gold coins. These in turn were replaced by the £1 Treasury note, then by the Bank of England £1 note, and then eventually by the £1 coin. In Scotland, of course, the three main banks still issue their notes of £5 and upwards, the £1 note having been discontinued except by the Royal Bank of Scotland.

My starting salary was £80 per annum, said to be the most generous pay of all the Scottish banks. It rose first by annual increments of £10, and later by £20, to the top of the scale, after which increases could be slow to come your way, and many appointments were more a matter of luck than of proven competence.

In the 1920s in a country branch, business was leisurely and uncomplicated. My duties were simple: opening (and closing) the doors, closing window shutters (I don't know why), taking out and putting back all books and ledgers. There was meticulous accuracy, no erasures – stroke out and insert – and all entries were by pen and ink. There were wearisome additions – 50-line columns in regular returns. How I envied some clerks I met later who could add three columns of figures in one operation and produce the correct answers first time – in pounds, shillings and pence. Later, when I was transferred to the Branch Department in Head Office where such returns came home to roost, I was shocked and disappointed to see some of our meticulous returns filed away in the strongroom with hardly a glance at their content.

We were open for business between 9.30 am and 3 pm. On many days when business was quiet, the accountant and I were sometimes balanced, with everything completed, by 3 o'clock and waiting for the town clock to strike. In summer that would release me for golf or fishing. In winter the two of us would resort to the billiards room in the Aros Hall for a few '100-ups'.

The winter leisure time allowed me more time for study at home by the soft lighting of the paraffin lamp and a warm fire. There were four years of this. First there were the compulsory examinations of the Institute of Banking in Scotland, then the voluntary equivalent in the English Institute. Thanks

The author playing the melodeon c. 1920

to the quiet environment and therefore ease of concentration, I had no difficulty in passing both examinations, with distinction in the English, but as far as I am aware this counted little towards advancement. Later in my career I lectured for a few years on the history of banking in Scotland to banking students. This taught them to have an extra pride in their heritage; that Scotland, a seemingly poor country in the past, had since 1696 the finest banking system in the world based on unfettered competition (unlike the dead hand of government in England that interfered through the monopoly of the Bank of England).

There were then eight Scottish banks, each with the right to issue its own notes. But no bank could use the notes of any other bank, and these had to be returned to the bank of issue through a local note exchange. In Tobermory there were only two banks, but we were obliged to accumulate the notes of the other banks until the holding became embarrassingly large, whereupon another of my duties arose which was to

The author in 1925

convey this safely to our Oban branch, where it could be passed to the other banks in the town. I was in sole charge of the priceless cargo, all roped and sealed along with our surplus copper and silver in a wooden box, thinly disguised by the stencilled notation 'One dozen bottles Old Mull Whisky'. I had to collect this from the bank early in the morning in time for the 7.30 am departure of the *Lochinvar*. I would hand the box to the purser who locked it in his office, with some reluctance, leaving me to grip convulsively a stout leather bag containing any banknotes that might not fit into the box.

On arrival at Oban pier I would catch the eye of the least un-prepossessing of the red-faced registered porters with their peaked caps – all gone long since – and accompany him and his barrow of riches to our Oban office, 'While peerin' round with prudent care'. A tip of 1/- was considered munificent, but after all, the bank was paying it. In winter this trip to Oban and back could be very dreary, but in summer it was a nice outing.

I remember one occasion in a busy Glasgow street chatting casually with a couple of colleagues from Head Office on our way to the note exchange building. We were following two bank messengers bowed down with a huge container holding over £100,000 in mixed used notes. There was not a guard or policeman in sight.

I once had to undertake another (fortunately one-off) job. In the bank in Tobermory there was a tiny strongroom which was overflowing with old records, particularly paid cheques – in the past a customer had to sign a form absolving us from all blame before we would part with his cheques. We had arranged with Head Office that we could get rid of these up to a certain date. I piled five sackloads of assorted paperwork into a rowing boat and, armed with plenty of matches, rowed round the coast to Port-a'Choit where I soon had an impressive blaze going on the rocky shore. Then the wind got up, and suddenly I was desperately chasing after a storm of fluttering cheques, any of which, and in particular those bearing the signatures of the most distinguished people in Mull, would have brought retaliation on the bank if it had fallen into the wrong hands, and of course on me in particular. Some of the cheques were dated back to the 1840s and bore the one penny Victorian stamp representing the then newly imposed duty on banknotes. Somehow or other, I managed to retrieve and dispose of the lot.

The annual inspection of the branch lasted for three days, which was the most the inspector could squeeze out of it. When the work was nearly over, I used to slip off to my favourite fishing haunt and return with a few nice trout which I presented to the inspector, who accepted them graciously. I hoped that would ease his report about the 3d. short in my postage book!

When customers came to town on their infrequent visits from distant corners of the island, they made a day of it! Ensconced in the agent's room, discussion would range far and wide – first the crops, then the family, other people, livestock

The author in 1926

and 'the Subsidy', before coming to the business in hand. As a result, the accountant and I might have to wait long after closing time before the agent was free to sign the daily letters and the returns, which we then had to make up and post.

Behind its veneer of super-respectability, banking has its humorous side. We had one customer who had come from the East of Scotland and was reputed to be the meanest person in the town. He lived by himself in a two-apartment flat. One day he was in the bank, laying off to the agent, and as the door was ajar, we heard the conversation. Aggressively he bellowed 'Aye, this brither-in law of mine would come an' stay a week wi' me, for he kent Ah had a spare bed. Ah soon stoppit that! Ah selt the bed!' Another time a man came in rather sheepishly and with great care unfolded a newspaper on the counter, revealing a heap of half-charred banknotes. 'What on earth has happened here?' we asked. 'Ach, well,' he replied, 'This was a nest egg the wife didn't know about, and I kept it hidden for safety in the best room under the grate that my wife never lights. Here, when I was out today, did she no' light a fire to air the room!' Unfortunately, we could reclaim for him only those notes that still had the cashier's signature and one of the numbers.

A former lawyer's clerk lived with his sister in a lonely house 'over the hill'. On her death he became peculiar, and when he died, it was found that he had been living all alone and neglected in one room which was littered with rubbish. Among it was a drift of tattered rat-and mouse-chewed banknotes taken by the vermin from where they had been hidden. The fragments were brought to us, and in our spare time we tried to piece together and reclaim what we could; but out of what we estimated must have been £2,000, only a few hundred were saved.

I commuted to work daily on an old bicycle with negligible brakes that I later learned caused some apprehension among the crofters and livestock along the two miles of road. The 10 mph speed limit post at the Burgh boundary was indeed a challenge. I used to freewheel down the (1 in 7 gradient) Eas Brae to gather enough momentum to reach the bank door without touching the pedals. My most memorable near-squeak was when going at top speed round the bend at the Distillery, I was confronted by a horse and cart broadside on delivering a load of peats. There was what seemed an impossibly small gap between the horse's nose and the stone wall, on the other side of which foamed the Tobermory River 20ft below, but with an inch of clearance on both sides I shot through.

My years of sophistication began when I was transferred

The author in motor cycling attire in 1926

to Head Office in the busy centre of Glasgow in 1928. I worked in an elite department where our chief ordered us to pack up at the stroke of 4 o'clock, and we departed to dirty looks from the less fortunate. Here I first handled a telephone, which I picked up as if it were a live adder. However, I was soon lording it over nervous colleagues at the other end who were reporting sins of omission or commission.

I invested most of my savings in a big 500cc OHV motor cycle which cost me £56 'on the road'. Not only did this facilitate my visits to Dunfermline, where my mother had by that time settled, but it increased my knowledge of the topography of Scotland that was to stand me in good stead later. But this type of investment was frowned upon by my superiors as being infra dig for a banker, even a junior! A story went the rounds which was attributed to a Head Office official high in the pecking order ... 'I believe there are some young men in the bank today who spend as much as two or even three shillings on a

Author with Ariel motorcycle in 1928

Saturday night's entertainment.' But once on the permanent staff, we had an assured future as long as we conformed to the accepted standards of bankers. Such dedication to duty is brought out in the poem by Harry Graham – with one tiny change:

'There's been an accident,' they said;
Your teller's cut in half – HE'S DEAD!'
'Indeed?' said Mr Jones, 'then please
Send me the half that has the keys!'

The Ceilidh

I've seen the Mod at Oban,
At Largs and Aberdeen,
With all the world attending,
from Gairloch to Loch Sween,
With songs would charm the blackbird
And ceilidhs all the night,
Oh, the folk I would be seeing
And the talk 'till morning light:
But the best I e'er attended
(Now, you'll maybe think me soft)
Was the night we held the ceilidh
up at Katie Crùpach's croft.

A byre for holding five or six,
Besides the hens and stirks;
A barn with ever-sagging roof,
Wherein a secret lurks;
For Katie's brother Donald,
Tho' hardly in his eighties,
A still he ran behind the barn;
Of course the plan was Katie's:
And "Donald's Wine" was all the rage,
A dram both smooth and heady,
In bottles of assorted makes
As soon as it was ready.

Old Mull and Grant's Glenfiddich,
Islay Mist and Ballantine –
It didn't really matter,
For the people liked it fine;
The gauger, when he had a glass,
Could hardly keep his feet;
There was nothing in his bond, he said,
That could with it compete,
And stacks of kegs and bottles
were hidden in the loft
For the night we held the ceilidh
up at Katie Crùpach's croft.

The music was by Piobaireachan,
with his enchanted fiddle,
And Johnny Squeezebox with his hair
all parted down the middle,
And Eachann Mor from Dervaig
would pipe the whole night through
On only just a pint or two
of Donald's "Mountain Dew".

We sang Farewell to Fiunary,
And then An t'Eilean Muileach
And a ho-ro-yally chorus
Led by little Callum Dulach'
Then Eachann Mòr set up his pipes
And blew with all his might;
The drones went roaring up the glen
And put the stags to flight.

The folk could hardly keep their seats,
But danced with might and main,
Even Katie and her brother
Hooched and set, and set again.
The young folk slipped out and in,
The moon was fair entrancing;
A corner of Kate Crùpach's corn
Was better than the dancing.
Then a drop or two of Donald's
To refresh the company,
Until the stack of bottles
Was reduced to two or three;
The empties that went down the burn
And floated far and near,
I'm sure from Port-a'Choit they reached
As far as Aros pier.

The sergeant and the Police patrol
Came up to show their paces;
Before we knew, the men in blue
Were dancing in their braces.
Now, eighteen stone (without his boots)
Was what the sergeant weighed;
The Highland Fling his specialty:
"Set up the pipes," he said.
As Eachann blew with all his breath
The sergeant danced with grace,
Then raised his hands above his head
As faster grew his pace;
At last he gave a mighty leap –
Oh, words could never tell

The things that happened in the barn
When through the floor he fell!
The roof came gently bending down;
The people roared with glee;
I'm sure we shifted half the floor
Before we pulled him free.

But now on Morvern's glowing hills
Had dawned another day.
In twos and threes the company
Began to wend their way,
With not a drop remaining,
As Donald sadly said,
So Katie gave them Beannachd Leat
And hirpled off to bed.

Pete Macnab

Some other books published by **LUATH** PRESS

FOLKLORE

Tall Tales from an Island

Peter Macnab

ISBN 0 946487 07 3 PBK £8.99

Peter Macnab was born and reared on Mull. He heard many of these tales as a lad, and others he has listened to in later years. Although collected on Mull, they could have come from any one of the Hebridean islands. Timeless and universal, these tales are still told round the fireside when the visitors have all gone home.

There are humorous tales, grim tales, witty tales, tales of witchcraft, tales of love, tales of heroism, tales of treachery, historical tales and tales of yesteryear. There are unforgettable characters like Do'l Gorm, the philosophical roadman, and Calum nan Croig, the Gaelic storyteller whose highly developed art of convincing exaggeration mesmerised his listeners. There is a headless horseman, and a whole coven of witches. Heroes, fools, lairds, herdsmen, lovers and liars, dead men and live cats all have a place in this entrancing collection. This is a superb collection indeed, told by a master storyteller with all the rhythms remembered from the firesides of his childhood.

A popular lecturer, broadcaster and writer, Peter Macnab is the author of a number of books and articles about Mull, the island he knows so intimately and loves so much. As he himself puts it in his introduction to this book 'I am of the unswerving opinion that nowhere else in the world will you find a better way of life, nor a finer people with whom to share it.'

'All islands, it seems, have a rich store of characters whose stories represent a kind of sub-culture without which island life would be that much poorer. Macnab has succeeded in giving the retelling of the stories a special Mull flavour, so much so that one can visualise the storytellers sitting on a bench outside the house with a few cronies, puffing on their pipes and listening with nodding approval.' WEST HIGHLAND FREE PRESS

The Supernatural Highlands

Francis Thompson

ISBN 0 946487 31 6 PBK £8.99

An authoritative exploration of the otherworld of the Highlander, happenings and beings hitherto thought to be outwith the ordinary forces of nature. A simple introduction to the way of life of rural Highland and Island communities, this new edition weaves a path through second sight, the evil eye, witchcraft, ghosts, fairies and other supernatural beings, offering new sight-lines on areas of belief once dismissed as folklore and superstition.

LUATH GUIDES TO SCOTLAND

These guides are not your traditional where-to-stay and what-to-eat books. They are companions in the rucksack or car seat, providing the discerning traveller with a blend of fiery opinion and moving description. Here you will find 'that curious pastiche of myths and legend and history that the Scots use to describe their heritage... what battle happened in which glen between which clans; where the Picts sacrificed bulls as recently as the 17th century... A lively counterpoint to the more standard, detached guidebook... Intriguing.' THE WASHINGTON POST

These are perfect guides for the discerning visitor or resident to keep close by for reading again and again, written by authors who invite you to share their intimate knowledge and love of the areas covered.

Highways and Byways in Mull and Iona

Peter Macnab
ISBN 0 946487 16 2 PBK £4.25
'The Isle of Mull is of Isles the fairest,
Of ocean's gems 'tis the first and rarest.'
So a local poet described it a hundred years ago, and this recently revised guide to Mull and sacred Iona, the most accessible islands of the Inner Hebrides, takes the reader on a delightful tour of these rare ocean gems, travelling with a native whose unparalleled knowledge and deep feeling for the area unlock the byways of the islands in all their natural beauty.

South West Scotland

Tom Atkinson
ISBN 0 946487 04 9 PBK £4.95
This descriptive guide to the magical country of Robert Burns covers Kyle, Carrick, Galloway, Dumfries-shire, Kirkcudbrightshire and Wigtownshire. Hills, unknown moors and unspoiled beaches grace a land steeped in history and legend and portrayed with affection and deep delight.
An essential book for the visitor who yearns to feel at home in this land of peace and grandeur.

The Lonely Lands

Tom Atkinson
ISBN 0 946487 10 3 PBK £4.95
A guide to Inveraray, Glencoe, Loch Awe, Loch Lomond, Cowal, the Kyles of Bute and all of central Argyll written with insight, sympathy and loving detail. Once Atkinson has taken you there, these lands can never feel lonely. 'I have sought to make the complex simple, the beautiful accessible and the strange familiar,' he writes, and indeed he brings to the land a knowledge and affection only accessible to someone with intimate knowledge of the area.
A must for travellers and natives who want to delve beneath the surface.
'Highly personal and somewhat quirky... steeped in the lore of Scotland.'
THE WASHINGTON POST

The Empty Lands

Tom Atkinson
ISBN 0 946487 13 8 PBK £4.95
The Highlands of Scotland from Ullapool to Bettyhill and Bonar Bridge to John O'Groats are landscapes of myth and legend, 'empty of people, but of nothing else that brings delight to any tired soul,' writes Atkinson. This highly personal guide describes Highland history and landscape with love, compassion and above all sheer magic.
Essential reading for anyone who has dreamed of the Highlands.

Roads to the Isles

Tom Atkinson
ISBN 0 946487 01 4 PBK £4.95
Ardnamurchan, Morvern, Morar, Moidart and the west coast to Ullapool are included in this guide to the Far West and Far North of Scotland. An unspoiled land of mountains, lochs and silver sands is brought to the walker's toe-tips (and to the reader's fingertips) in this stark,

serene and evocative account of town, country and legend.

For any visitor to this Highland wonderland, Queen Victoria's favourite place on earth.

NATURAL SCOTLAND

Rum: Nature's Island

Magnus Magnusson

ISBN 0 946487 32 4   £7.95 PBK

Rum: Nature's Island is the fascinating story of a Hebridean island from the earliest times through to the Clearances and its period as the sporting playground of a Lancashire industrial magnate, and on to its rebirth as a National Nature Reserve, a model for the active ecological management of Scotland's wild places.

Thoroughly researched and written in a lively accessible style, the book includes comprehensive coverage of the island's geology, animals and plants, and people, with a special chapter on the Edwardian extravaganza of Kinloch Castle. There is practical information for visitors to what was once known as 'the Forbidden Isle'; the book provides details of bothy and other accommodation, walks and nature trails. It closes with a positive vision for the island's future: biologically diverse, economically dynamic and ecologically sustainable.

Rum: Nature's Island is published in co-operation with Scottish Natural Heritage (of which Magnus Magnusson is Chairman) to mark the 40th anniversary of the acquisition of Rum by its predecessor, The Nature Conservancy.

Wild Scotland: The essential guide to finding the best of natural Scotland

James McCarthy

Photography by Laurie Campbell

ISBN 0 946487 37 5   PBK £7.50

With a foreword by Magnus Magnus-son and striking colour photographs by Laurie Campbell, this is the essential up-to-date guide to viewing wildlife in Scotland for the visitor and resident alike. It provides a fascinating overview of the country's plants, animals, bird and marine life against the background of their typical natural settings, as an introduction to the vivid descriptions of the most accessible localities, linked to clear regional maps. A unique feature is the focus on 'green tourism' and sustainable visitor use of the countryside, contributed by Duncan Bryden, manager of the Scottish Tourist Board's Tourism and the Environment Task Force. Important practical information on access and the best times of year for viewing sites makes this an indispensable and user-friendly travelling companion to anyone interested in exploring Scotland's remarkable natural heritage.

James McCarthy is former Deputy Director for Scotland of the Nature Conservancy Council, and now a Board Member of Scottish Natural Heritage and Chairman of the Environmental Youth Work National Development Project Scotland.

An Inhabited Solitude: Scotland – Land and People

James McCarthy

ISBN 0 946487 30 8 PBK £6.99

'Scotland is the country above all others that I have seen, in which a man of imagination may carve out his own pleasures; there are so many inhabited solitudes.'

DOROTHY WORDSWORTH, in her journal of August 1803

An informed and thought-provoking profile of Scotland's unique landscapes and the impact of humans on what we see now and in the future. James McCarthy leads us through the many aspects of the land and the people who inhabit it: natural Scotland; the rocks beneath; land ownership; the use of resources; people and place; conserving Scotland's heritage and much more.

Written in a highly readable style, this concise volume offers an understanding of the land as a whole. Emphasising the uniqueness of the Scottish environment, the author explores the links between this and other aspects of our culture as a key element in rediscovering a modern sense of the Scottish identity and perception of nationhood.

'This book provides an engaging introduction to the mysteries of Scotland's people and landscapes. Difficult concepts are described in simple terms, providing the interested Scot or tourist with an invaluable overview of the country... It fills an important niche which, to my knowledge, is filled by no other publications.'

BETSY KING, Chief Executive, Scottish Environmental Education Council.

The Highland Geology Trail

John L Roberts

ISBN 0946487 36 7   PBK £4.99

Where can you find the oldest rocks in Europe?

Where can you see ancient hills around 800 million years old?

How do you tell whether a valley was carved out by a glacier, not a river?

What are the Fucoid Beds?

Where do you find rocks folded like putty?

How did great masses of rock pile up like snow in front of a snow-plough?

When did volcanoes spew lava and ash to form Skye, Mull and Rum?

Where can you find fossils on Skye?

'...a lucid introduction to the geological record in general, a jargon-free exposition of the regional background, and a series of descriptions of specific localities of geological interest on a "trail" around the highlands.

Having checked out the local references on the ground, I can vouch for their accuracy and

look forward to investigating farther afield, informed by this guide.

Great care has been taken to explain specific terms as they occur and, in so doing, John Roberts has created a resource of great value which is eminently usable by anyone with an interest in the outdoors...the best bargain you are likely to get as a geology book in the foreseeable future.'

Jim Johnston, PRESS AND JOURNAL

WALK WITH LUATH
Mountain Days & Bothy Nights

Dave Brown and Ian Mitchell

ISBN 0 946487 15 4   PBK £7.50

Acknowledged as a classic of mountain writing still in demand ten years after its first publication, this book takes you into the bothies, howffs and dosses on the Scottish hills. Fishgut Mac, Desperate Dan and Stumpy the Big Yin stalk hill and public house, evading gamekeepers and Royalty with a camaraderie which was the trademark of Scots hillwalking in the early days.

'The fun element comes through... how innocent the social polemic seems in our nastier world of today... the book for the rucksack this year.'

Hamish Brown, SCOTTISH MOUNTAINEERING CLUB JOURNAL

'The doings, sayings, incongruities and idiosyncrasies of the denizens of the bothy underworld... described in an easy philosophical style... an authentic word picture of this part of the climbing scene in latter-day Scotland, which, like any good picture, will increase in charm over the years.'

Iain Smart, SCOTTISH MOUNTAINEERING CLUB JOURNAL

'The ideal book for nostalgic hillwalkers of the 60s, even just the armchair and public house variety... humorous, entertaining, informative, written by two men with obvious expertise, knowledge and love of their subject.'

SCOTS INDEPENDENT

'Fifty years have made no difference. Your crowd is the one I used to know... [This] must be the only complete dossers' guide ever put together.'

Alistair Borthwick, author of the immortal *Always a Little Further.*

The Joy of Hillwalking

Ralph Storer

ISBN 0 946487 28 6 PBK £7.50

Apart, perhaps, from the joy of sex, the joy of hillwalking brings more pleasure to more people than any other form of human activity.

'Alps, America, Scandinavia, you name it – Storer's been there, so why the hell shouldn't he bring all these various and varied places into his observations... [He] even admits to losing his virginity after a day on the Aggy Ridge... Well worth its place alongside Storer's earlier works.'

TAC

Scotland's Mountains before the Mountaineers

Ian Mitchell

ISBN 0 946487 39 1 PBK £9.99

How many Munros did Bonnie Prince Charlie bag?

Which clergyman climbed all the Cairngorm 4,000-ers nearly two centuries ago?

Which bandit and sheep rustler hid in the mountains while his wife saw off the sheriff officers with a shotgun?

According to Gaelic tradition, how did an outlier of the rugged Corbett Beinn Aridh Charr come to be called Spidean Moirich, 'Martha's Peak'?

Who was the murderous clansman who gave his name to Beinn Fhionnlaidh?

In this ground-breaking book, Ian Mitchell tells the story of explorations and ascents in the Scottish Highlands in the days before mountaineering became a

popular sport - when bandits, Jacobites, poachers and illicit distillers traditionally used the mountains as sanctuary. The book also gives a detailed account of the map makers, road builders, geologists, astronomers and naturalists, many of whom ascended hitherto untrodden summits while working in the Scottish Highlands.

Scotland's Mountains before Mountaineers is divided into four Highland regions, with a map of each region showing key summits. While not designed primarily as a guide, it will be a useful handbook for walkers and climbers. Based on a wealth of new research, this book offers a fresh perspective that will fascinate climbers and mountaineers and everyone interested in the history of mountaineering, cartography, the evolution of landscape and the social history of the Scottish Highlands.

LUATH WALKING GUIDES

The highly respected and continually updated guides to the Cairngorms.

'Particularly good on local wildlife and how to see it'

THE COUNTRYMAN

Walks in the Cairngorms

Ernest Cross

ISBN 0 946487 09 X PBK £3.95

This selection of walks celebrates the rare birds, animals, plants and geological wonders of a region often believed difficult to penetrate on foot. Nothing is difficult with this guide in your pocket, as Cross gives a choice for every walker, and includes valuable tips on mountain safety and weather advice.

Ideal for walkers of all ages and skiers waiting for snowier skies.

Short Walks in the Cairngorms

Ernest Cross

ISBN 0 946487 23 5 PBK £3.95

Cross wrote this volume after overhearing a walker remark that there were no short walks for lazy ramblers in the Cairngorm region. Here is the answer: rambles through scenic woods with a welcoming pub at the end, birdwatching hints, glacier holes, or for the fit and ambitious, scrambles up hills to admire vistas of glorious scenery. Wildlife in the Cairngorms is unequalled elsewhere in Britain, and here it is brought to the binoculars of any walker who treads quietly and with respect.

SPORT

Over the Top with the Tartan Army (Active Service 1992-97)

Andrew McArthur

ISBN 0 946487 45 6 PBK £7.99

Scotland has witnessed the growth of a new and curious military phenomenon - grown men bedecked in tartan yomping across the globe, hell-bent on benevolence and ritualistic bevvying. What noble cause does this famous army serve? Why, football of course!

Taking us on an erratic world tour, McArthur gives a frighteningly funny insider's eye view of active service with the Tartan Army - the madcap antics of Scotland's travelling support in the '90s, written from the inside, covering campaigns and skirmishes from Euro '92 up to the qualifying drama for France '98 in places as diverse as Russia, the Faroes, Belarus, Sweden, Monte Carlo, Estonia, Latvia, USA and Finland.

This book is a must for any football fan who likes a good laugh.

'I commend this book to all football supporters'. Graham Spiers, SCOTLAND ON SUNDAY

'In wishing Andy McArthur all the best with this publication, I do hope he will be in a position to produce a sequel after our participation in the World Cup in France.

CRAIG BROWN, Scotland Team Coach

All royalties on sales of the book are going to Scottish charities, principally Children's Hospice Association Scotland, the only Scotland-wide charity of its kind, providing special love and care to children with terminal illnesses at its hospice, Rachel House, in Kinross.

Ski & Snowboard Scotland

Hilary Parke

ISBN 0 946487 35 9 PBK £6.99

How can you cut down the queue time and boost the snow time?

Who can show you how to cannonball the quarterpipe?

Where are the bumps that give most airtime?

Where can you watch international rugby in-between runs on the slopes?

Which mountain restaurant serves magical Mexican meals?

Which resort has the steepest on-piste run in Scotland?

Where can you get a free ski guiding service to show you the best runs?

If you don't know the answers to all these questions - plus a hundred or so more then this book is for you!

Snow sports in Scotland are still a secret treasure. There's no need to go abroad when there's such an exciting variety of terrain right here on your doorstep. You just need to know what to look for. Ski & Snowboard Scotland is aimed at maximising the time you have available so that the hours you spend on the snow are memorable for all the right reasons. This fun and informative book guides you over the slopes of Scotland, giving you the inside track on all the major ski centres. There are chapters ranging from how to get there to the impact of snowsports on the environment.

'Reading the book brought back many happy memories of my early training days at the dry slope in Edinburgh and of many brilliant weekends in the Cairngorms.'

EMMA CARRICK-ANDERSON, from her foreword, written in the US, during a break in training for her first World Cup as a member of the British Alpine Ski Team.

SOCIAL HISTORY

The Crofting Years

Francis Thompson

ISBN 0 946487 06 5 PBK £6.95

Crofting is much more than a way of life. It is a storehouse of cultural, linguistic and moral values which holds together a scattered and struggling rural population. This book fills a blank in the written history of crofting over the last two centuries. Bloody conflicts and gunboat diplomacy, treachery, compassion, music and story: all figure in this mine of information on crofting in the Highlands and Islands of Scotland.

'I would recommend this book to all who are interested in the past, but even more so to those who are interested in the future survival of our way of life and culture' STORNOWAY GAZETTE

'A cleverly planned book... the story told in simple words which compel attention... [by] a Gaelic speaking Lewisman with specialised knowledge of the crofting community.'
BOOKS IN SCOTLAND

'The book is a mine of information on many aspects of the past, among them the homes, the food, the music and the medicine of our crofting forebears.'
John M Macmillan, erstwhile CROFTERS COMMISSIONER FOR LEWIS AND HARRIS

'This fascinating book is recommended to

anyone who has the interests of our language and culture at heart.'
Donnie Maclean, DIRECTOR OF AN COMUNN GAIDHEALACH, WESTERN ISLES

'Unlike many books on the subject, Crofting Years combines a radical political approach to Scottish crofting experience with a ruthless realism which while recognising the full tragedy and difficulty of his subject never descends to sentimentality or nostalgia'
CHAPMAN

MUSIC AND DANCE

Highland Balls and Village Halls

GW Lockhart

ISBN 0 946487 12 X PBK £6.95

Acknowledged as a classic in Scottish dancing circles throughout the world. Anecdotes, Scottish history, dress and dance steps are all included in this

'delightful little book, full of interest... both a personal account and an understanding look at the making of traditions.'
NEW ZEALAND SCOTTISH COUNTRY DANCES MAGAZINE

'A delightful survey of Scottish dancing and custom. Informative, concise and opinionated, it guides the reader across the history and geography of country dance and ends by detailing the 12 dances every Scot should know – the most famous being the Eightsome Reel, "the greatest longest, rowdiest, most diabolically executed of all the Scottish country dances".'
THE HERALD

'A pot-pourri of every facet of Scottish country dancing. It will bring back memories of petronella turns and poussettes and make you eager to take part in a Broun's reel or a dashing white sergeant!'
DUNDEE COURIER AND ADVERTISER

'An excellent an very readable insight into

the traditions and customs of Scottish country dancing. The author takes us on a tour from his own early days jigging in the village hall to the characters and traditions that have made our own brand of dance popular throughout the world.'
SUNDAY POST

Fiddles & Folk: A celebration of the re-emergence of Scotland's musical heritage

GW Lockhart
ISBN 0 946487 38 3 PBK £7.95

In *Fiddles & Folk*, his companion volume to *Highland Balls and Village Halls*, now an acknowledged classic on Scottish dancing, Wallace Lockhart meets up with many of the people who have created the renaissance of Scotlandís music at home and overseas.

From Dougie MacLean, Hamish Henderson, the Battlefield Band, the Whistlebinkies, the Scottish Fiddle Orchestra, the McCalmans and many more come the stories that break down the musical barriers between Scotland's past and present, and between the diverse musical forms which have woven together to create the dynamism of the music today.

'I have tried to avoid a formal approach to Scottish music as it affects those of us with our musical heritage coursing through our veins. The picture I have sought is one of many brush strokes, looking at how some individuals have come to the fore, examining their music, lives, thoughts, even philosophies...' WALLACE LOCKHART

' *"I never had a narrow, woolly-jumper, fingers stuck in the ear approach to music. We have a musical heritage here that is the envy of the rest of the world. Most countries just can't compete,"* he *[Ian Green, Greentrax] says. And as young Scots tire of Oasis and Blur, they will realise that there is*

a wealth of young Scottish music on their doorstep just waiting to be discovered.' THE SCOTSMAN, March 1998

For anyone whose heart lifts at the sound of fiddle or pipes, this book takes you on a delightful journey, full of humour and respect, in the company of some of the performers who have taken Scotland's music around the world and come back enriched.

FICTION

The Bannockburn Years

William Scott
ISBN 0 946487 34 0 PBK £7.95

A present day Edinburgh solicitor stumbles across reference to a document of value to the Nation State of Scotland. He tracks down the document on the Isle of Bute, a document which probes the real 'quaestiones' about nationhood and national identity. The document ends up being published, but is it authentic and does it matter? Almost 700 years on, these 'quaestiones' are still worth asking.

Written with pace and passion, William Scott has devised an intriguing vehicle to open up new ways of looking at the future of Scotland and its people. He presents an alternative interpretation of how the Battle of Bannockburn was fought, and through the Bannatyne manuscript he draws the reader into the minds of those involved.

Winner of the 1997 Constable Trophy, the premier award in Scotland for an unpublished novel, this book offers new insights to both the academic and the general reader which are sure to provoke further discussion and debate.

'A brilliant storyteller. I shall expect to see your name writ large hereafter.'
NIGEL TRANTER, October 1997.

'... a compulsive read.' PH Scott, THE SCOTSMASN

The Great Melnikov

Hugh MacLachlan

ISBN 0 946487 42 1 PBK £7.95

A well crafted, gripping novel, written in a style reminiscent of John Buchan and set in London and the Scottish Highlands during the First World War, *The Great Melnikov* is a dark tale of double-cross and deception. We first meet Melnikov, one-time star of the German circus, languishing as a down-and-out in Trafalgar Square. He soon finds himself drawn into a tortuous web of intrigue. He is a complex man whose personal struggle with alcoholism is an inner drama which parallels the tense twists and turns of the spy mystery which unfolds. Melnikov's options are narrowing. The circle of threat is closing. Will Melnikov outwit the sinister enemy spy network? Can he summon the will and the wit to survive?

Hugh MacLachlan, in his first full length novel, demonstrates an undoubted ability to tell a good story well. His earlier stories have been broadcast on Radio Scotland, and he has the rare distinction of having been shortlisted for the Macallan/Scotland on Sunday Short Story Competition two years in succession.

BIOGRAPHY

Bare Feet and Tackety Boots

Archie Cameron

ISBN 0 946487 17 0 PBK £7.95

The island of Rum before the First World War was the playground of its rich absentee landowner. A survivor of life a century gone tells his story. Factors and schoolmasters, midges and poaching, deer, ducks and MacBrayne's steamers: here social history and personal anecdote create a record of a way of life gone not long ago but already almost forgotten. This is the story the gentry couldn't tell.

'This book is an important piece of social history, for it gives an insight into how the other half lived in an era the likes of which will never be seen again'
FORTHRIGHT MAGAZINE

'The authentic breath of the pawky, country-wise estate employee.'
THE OBSERVER

'Well observed and detailed account of island life in the early years of this century'.
THE SCOTS MAGAZINE

'A very good read with the capacity to make the reader chuckle. A very talented writer.'
STORNOWAY GAZETTE

On the Trail of Robert Service

GW Lockhart

ISBN 0 946487 24 3 PBK £7.99

Robert Service is famed world-wide for his eye-witness verse-pictures of the Klondike goldrush. As a war poet, his work outsold Owen and Sassoon, and he went on to become the world's first million selling poet. In search of adventure and new experiences, he emigrated from Scotland to Canada in 1890 where he was caught up in the aftermath of the raging gold fever. His vivid dramatic verse bring to life the wild, larger than life characters of the gold rush Yukon, their bar-room brawls, their lust for gold, their trigger-happy gambles with life and love. 'The Shooting of Dan McGrew' is perhaps his most famous poem:

A bunch of the boys were whooping it up in the Malamute saloon;
The kid that handles the music box was hitting a ragtime tune;
Back of the bar in a solo game, sat Dangerous Dan McGrew,
And watching his luck was his light o'love, the lady that's known as Lou.

His storytelling powers have brought Robert Service enduring fame, particularly in North America and Scotland where he is something of a cult figure.

Starting in Scotland, *On the Trail of Robert Service* follows Service as he wanders through British Columbia, Oregon, California, Mexico, Cuba, Tahiti, Russia, Turkey and the Balkans, finally 'settling' in France.

This revised edition includes an expanded selection of illustrations of scenes from the Klondike as well as several photographs from the family of ·Robert Service on his travels around the world.

Wallace Lockhart, an expert on Scottish traditional folk music and dance, is the author of *Highland Balls & Village Halls* and *Fiddles & Folk*. His relish for a well-told tale in popular vernacular led him to fall in love with the verse of Robert Service and write his biography.

'*A fitting tribute to a remarkable man - a bank clerk who wanted to become a cowboy. It is hard to imagine a bank clerk writing such lines as:*

A bunch of boys were whooping it up...

The income from his writing actually exceeded his bank salary by a factor of five and he resigned to pursue a full time writing career.' Charles Munn,

THE SCOTTISH BANKER

'*Robert Service claimed he wrote for those who wouldnit be seen dead reading poetry. His was an almost unbelievably mobile life... Lockhart hangs on breathlessly, enthusiastically unearthing clues to the poet's life.*' Ruth Thomas, SCOTTISH BOOK COLLECTOR

'*This enthralling biography will delight Service lovers in both the Old World and the New.*' Marilyn Wright, SCOTS INDEPENDENT

Come Dungeons Dark

John Taylor Caldwell
ISBN 0 946487 19 7 PBK £6.95
Glasgow anarchist Guy Aldred died with 10p in his pocket in 1963 claiming there was better company in Barlinnie Prison

than in the Corridors of Power. 'The Red Scourge' is remembered here by one who worked with him and spent 27 years as part of his turbulent household, sparring with Lenin, Sylvia Pankhurst and others as he struggled for freedom for his beloved fellow-man.

'*The welcome and long-awaited biography of... one of this country's most prolific radical propagandists... Crank or visionary?... whatever the verdict, the Glasgow anarchist has finally been given a fitting memorial.*'

THE SCOTSMAN

POETRY

Blind Harry's Wallace

William Hamilton of Gilbertfield
ISBN 0 946487 43 X HBK £15.00
ISBN 0 946487 33 2 PBK £7.50
The original story of the real braveheart, Sir William Wallace. Racy, blood on every page, violently anglophobic, grossly embellished, vulgar and disgusting, clumsy and stilted, a literary failure, a great epic.

Whatever the verdict on BLIND HARRY, this is the book which has done more than any other to frame the notion of Scotland's national identity. Despite its numerous 'historical inaccuracies', it remains the principal source for what we now know about the life of Wallace.

The novel and film *Braveheart* were based on the 1722 Hamilton edition of this epic poem. Burns, Wordsworth, Byron and others were greatly influenced by this version 'wherein the old obsolete words are rendered more intelligible', which is said to be the book, next to the Bible, most commonly found in Scottish households in the eighteenth century. Burns even admits to having 'borrowed... a couplet worthy of Homer' directly from Hamilton's version of BLIND HARRY to include in '*Scots wha hae*'.

Elspeth King, in her introduction to this, the first accessible edition of BLIND HARRY in verse form since 1859, draws parallels between the situation in Scotland at the time of Wallace and that in Bosnia and Chechnya in the 1990s. Seven hundred years to the day after the Battle of Stirling Bridge, the 'Settled Will of the Scottish People' was expressed in the devolution referendum of 11 September 1997. She describes this as a landmark opportunity for mature reflection on how the nation has been shaped, and sees BLIND HARRY'S WALLACE as an essential and compelling text for this purpose.

'Builder of the literary foundations of a national hero-cult in a free and powerful country'.

ALEXANDER STODDART, sculptor

'A true bard of the people'

TOM SCOTT, THE PENGUIN BOOK OF SCOTTISH VERSE, on Blind Harry.

'A more inventive writer than Shakespeare'

RANDALL WALLACE

'The story of Wallace poured a Scottish prejudice in my veins which will boil along until the floodgates of life shut in eternal rest'

ROBERT BURNS

'Hamilton's couplets are not the best poetry you will ever read, but they rattle along at a fair pace. In re-issuing this work, the publishers have re-opened the spring from which most of our conceptions of the Wallace legend come'.

SCOTLAND ON SUNDAY

'The return of Blind Harry's Wallace, a man who makes Mel look like a wimp'.

THE SCOTSMAN

Poems to be read aloud

Collected and with an introduction by Tom Atkinson

ISBN 0 946487 00 6 PBK £5.00

This personal collection of doggerel and verse ranging from the tear-jerking *Green Eye of the Yellow God* to the rarely printed, bawdy *Eskimo Nell* has a lively cult following. Much borrowed and rarely returned, this is a book for reading aloud in very good company, preferably after a dram or twa. You are guaranteed a warm welcome if you arrive at a gathering with this little volume in your pocket.

This little book is an attempt to stem the great rushing tide of canned entertainment. A hopeless attempt of course. There is poetry of very high order here, but there is also some fearful doggerel. But that is the way of things. No literary axe is being ground.

Of course some of the items in this book are poetic drivel, if read as poems. But that is not the point. They all spring to life when they are read aloud. It is the combination of the poem with your voice, with all the art and craft you can muster, that produces the finished product and effect you seek.

You don't have to learn the poems. Why clutter up your mind with rubbish? Of course, it is a poorly furnished mind that doesn't carry a fair stock of poetry, but surely the poems to be remembered and savoured in secret, when in love, or ill, or sad, are not the ones you want to share with an audience.

So go ahead, clear your throat and transfix all talkers with a stern eye, then let rip! TOM ATKINSON

Luath Press Limited
committed to publishing well written books worth reading

LUATH PRESS takes its name from Robert Burns, whose little collie Luath (*Gael.,* swift or nimble) tripped up Jean Armour at a wedding and gave him the chance to speak to the woman who was to be his wife and the abiding love of his life. Burns called one of *The Twa Dogs* Luath after Cuchullin's hunting dog in *Ossian's Fingal.* Luath Press grew up in the heart of Burns country, and now resides a few steps up the road from Burns' first lodgings in Edinburgh's Royal Mile.
Luath offers you distinctive writing with a hint of unexpected pleasures.

Most UK bookshops either carry our books in stock or can order them for you. To order direct from us, please send a £sterling cheque, postal order, international money order or your credit card details (number, address of cardholder and expiry date) to us at the address below. Please add post and packing as follows: UK – £1.00 per delivery address; overseas surface mail – £2.50 per delivery address; overseas airmail – £3.50 for the first book to each delivery address, plus £1.00 for each additional book by airmail to the same address. If your order is a gift, we will happily enclose your card or message at no extra charge.

Luath Press Limited
543/2 Castlehill
The Royal Mile
Edinburgh EH1 2ND
Telephone: 0131 225 4326 (24 hours)
Fax: 0131 225 4324
email: gavin.macdougall@luath.co.uk
Website: www.luath.co.uk